SACRED ROOTS SPIRITUAL CLASSICS

"Toward Ten Thousand Tozers"

On the Incarnation:
The Good News of Jesus for the Renewal of the World

SACRED ROOTS SPIRITUAL CLASSICS 6

Athanasius of Alexandria
edited by
Jeremy Treat

On the Incarnation: The Good News of Jesus for the Renewal of the World

© 2025. Samuel Morris Publications. All Rights Reserved.

ISBN: 978-1-955424-32-5

Copying, redistribution and/or sale of these materials, or any unauthorized transmission, except as may be expressly permitted by the 1976 Copyright Act or in writing from the publisher is prohibited. Requests for permission should be addressed in writing.

Published jointly in 2025 by TUMI Press and Samuel Morris Publications.

TUMI Press is a division of World Impact, Inc.

> TUMI Press
> The Urban Ministry Institute
> 3701 E. 13th Street, Suite 100
> Wichita, KS 67208

Equipping Leaders. Empowering Movements.

Samuel Morris Publications:

> Samuel Morris Publications
> Sacred Roots Project at Taylor University
> 1846 S Main Street
> Upland, IN 46989

Samuel Morris Publications publishes texts in service to the evangelical church's life together and its ongoing pursuit of a deeper conformity to Jesus Christ (Galatians 4:19).

All Scripture quotations, unless otherwise noted, are taken from The Holy Bible, English Standard Version, copyright © 2001 by Crossway Bible, a division of Good News Publishers. Used by permission. All Rights Reserved.

Appendix 2 is reprinted with permission from Athanasius, *Letter to Marcellinus on the Psalms: Spiritual Wisdom for Today*, trans. Joel C. Elowsky (New Haven, CT: ICCS Press, 2021).

For more information about Sacred Roots visit sacredrootsministry.org.

What "They" Say ... What Will You Say?

Athanasius's *On the Incarnation* is one of the preeminent classics in Christian history, worthy of continual introduction and reintroduction to the church. I am grateful that this edition will keep Athanasius at the front of people's minds, with a helpful introduction by Jeremy Treat as an added bonus.

~ **Brandon D. Smith, PhD**
Associate Professor of Theology & Early Christianity
Cofounder of the Center for Baptist Renewal
Oklahoma Baptist University

If I had the power to make every Christian, every church, every small group, and every Sunday school class read Athanasius's *On the Incarnation*, I would do it. This project gets us a little closer to that goal. I cannot imagine a more important book for our current cultural moment. This book represents the best of innovative theology and theological retrieval. In other words, the church needs to keep saying the same thing in new ways. I'm praying this book gets a wide reading.

~ **J. T. English, PhD**
Lead Pastor, Storyline Church
Associate Professor of Christian Theology,
The Southern Baptist Theological Seminary

In our distracted age, we have difficulty seeing how things hold together. We are scattered in thought, word, and deed, and we need to be made whole again. I don't know that anyone has written more beautifully or truthfully of how God has made us whole in Christ than Athanasius. He meditates on and marvels at the way in which Creator has renewed his image in creation, not by scrapping the project and starting over but by becoming a part of it and transforming it from within. Jeremy Treat's editorial work, especially in the way he frames discussion questions, brings this old book within reach of those of us who desperately need to hear good news of all God is making new.

~ **Matt Jenson, PhD**
Professor of Theology, Torrey Honors College, Biola University

Table of Contents

Series Preface vii

Acknowledgments xi

Introduction 1

Chapter 1
Creation as the Foundation of Salvation 23

Chapter 2
Human Sin and the Divine Dilemma 31

Chapter 3
The Incarnation as the Divine Solution 39

Chapter 4
The Death of Christ 59

Chapter 5
The Resurrection of Christ 71

Chapter 6
Refutation of the Jews 83

Chapter 7
Refutation of the Gentiles 99

Chapter 8
Living to the Glory of God. 123

Appendix 1
The Life of Antony. 127

Appendix 2
On the Psalms. 151

Afterword 175

Resources for Application 179

   Soul Work and Soul Care: Experiencing Renewal
   in Christ through a Simple and Disciplined Life . . 181

   Continuing the Conversation 187

   Glossary 189

   Map of Important Places: Athanasius of Alexandria . 191

   A Letter to God's Friends and Fellow Warriors On Why
   We Read the Sacred Roots Spiritual Classics Together . 192

   The Nicene Creed with Scriptural Support 208

   From Before to Beyond Time:
   The Plan of God and Human History 212

   About the Sacred Roots Project 215

Scripture Index 221

Series Preface

Christian spiritual classics are non-canonical texts testified to across centuries and cultures as helpful for soul work and soul care. While spiritual classics are not on the same level as Scripture, they are *deep* and *wide* texts written by master practitioners in the way of Jesus. These texts have stood the test of time (*deep*), having been read by Christian leaders for many decades or even centuries. These classics have also been read with profit across many cultures (*wide*). When apprenticing themselves to these wise authors, Christian leaders across many generations and diverse cultures have found themselves helped with nurturing their own souls and caring for the souls of others.

Sacred Roots Spiritual Classics equip urban, rural, and incarcerated congregational leaders with the wealth of the Christian tradition. In partnership with The Urban Ministry Institute (TUMI), each Sacred Roots Spiritual Classic is divided into eight chapters to correspond to TUMI's Capstone Curriculum modules (www.tumi.org). Additionally, each Sacred Roots Spiritual Classic is assigned a specific subject area within TUMI's Capstone Curriculum: Biblical Studies (red cover), Theology and Ethics (blue cover), Christian Ministry (orange cover), or Global Mission (purple cover). For a more detailed description, see the appendix "A Letter to God's Friends and Fellow Warriors on Why We Read the Sacred Roots Spiritual Classics Together."

Every Sacred Roots Spiritual Classic is edited by a scholar who has engaged it both academically and devotionally. The editor provides an introduction as well as chapter summaries. Each chapter consists of the actual text of the spiritual classic written by its author, not the editor, and concludes with five discussion questions to help you discuss the text with spiritual friends. Following chapters 1–8 is a summary afterword from the editor. Every classic also includes a "Continuing the Conversation" appendix with suggested resources, including other books written by the author, biographies, and more.

In chapters 1–8, the editor has either updated the old English to more contemporary English or provided a new translation. Additionally, the editor has added footnotes to define difficult or key vocabulary. The editor has also updated direct Scripture quotations to (usually) the English Standard Version, added Scripture references, and added italicized Scripture references to paraphrases of Scripture.

Before reading a Sacred Roots Spiritual Classic, we recommend you read both the classic's introduction and its "Soul Work and Soul Care" appendix. The latter offers practical suggestions for how to begin applying lessons from the spiritual classic into your life and ministry. Because many of the practices introduced in the spiritual classics may be new to readers, it can help to first understand some of the potential payoffs for investing in reading the spiritual classic before you begin.

Sacred Roots Spiritual Classics are available as paperbacks, hardbacks, e-books, and audiobooks. Additional resources for study and group discussion for each classic are available at www.sacredrootsministry.org.

THEOLOGY & ETHICS

Acknowledgments

Reading a book that is around seventeen hundred years old makes me realize that I am a part of something so much bigger than myself. Jesus lived, died, and rose from the grave, and then sent his followers to make disciples of all nations. Their message reached the people of Egypt (including Athanasius) and the people of America (including me). My life is a result of God's work through many generations and cultures, and for that I am incredibly grateful.

My gratitude extends not only to those in the past who have impacted my life, but also to those who make me who I am today. My wife, Tiffany, is my best friend and the greatest source of encouragement and support in my life. My daughters—Ashlyn, Lauryn, Evelyn, and Katelyn—bring me an abundance of joy. I love you all.

Hank Voss is one of my dearest friends, and I am so grateful for his constant encouragement for me to do this project. Isaiah Swain has been a reliable guide from beginning to end. Colin Davis put in hard work in helping me throughout. Thank you all.

I dedicate this book to my father- and mother-in-law, Terry and Anita Field. This is a book about renewal in Christ in the context of passing the faith from one generation to the next. That is exactly what you have done with your lives, as parents and grandparents. I love you both and will be forever grateful for the way you have impacted my life and our family for generations to come.

Introduction

Athanasius's *On the Incarnation* is my favorite book of all time. I will never forget the first time I read it in seminary. Having recently acquired a hunger to learn, I was devouring all the most popular books of the day about Jesus. As I opened *On the Incarnation*, I assumed that because it was around seventeen hundred years old that it would be stale and a step behind contemporary theology. But what I read not only corrected me but left me in awe. Athanasius declared the life, death, and resurrection of Jesus with as much depth as anything I had read, while at the same time adding more color to the gospel and doing so in a way that was pastoral, poetic, and yet concise. Furthermore, as I learned about Athanasius, I found relief that he was writing not from a posh cottage in the countryside but rather out of his life experience which was characterized by controversy and suffering. This was theology for real life. Athanasius's writing impacted me so much that I decided to read *On the Incarnation* every year around Christmas. As I have done so, each year my understanding of the person and work of Christ deepens and my love for God grows.

The Life of Athanasius

Athanasius was born around AD 296 in North Africa in the city of Alexandria.[1] The name "Athanasius" is Greek and means "immortal," which is a fitting name considering what would become of his theology and legacy. Although Athanasius did not grow up in a Christian home, he became a follower of Jesus early in life and was baptized along with his mother. Legend has it that Athanasius was playing on the beach, pretending to be the apostle Peter, when Alexander (the bishop of Alexandria) saw him playing and invited the young Athanasius to be his student. Athanasius would grow into a young man under Alexander's training and eventually accompany the bishop to the Council of Nicaea in AD 325.

While the Council of Nicaea would be the most important council in the history of the church, it began as an in-house squabble between Egyptian church leaders. Arius, a dynamic priest in Alexandria, taught that Jesus was not eternally the son of God but rather was created by God. Bishop Alexander strongly disagreed and argued from Scripture that Jesus has always been the Son of God and is therefore coeternal with the Father. The teachings of Arius, however, grew into a widespread movement known as Arianism, and began to influence Christians throughout the Roman Empire. When division became unbearable, Roman Emperor Constantine (who had recently converted to Christianity) called for a council to bring unity throughout the church and the empire.

---

1   Scholars agree Athanasius was born sometime between AD 295–299, although the exact year is disputed. Many details of Athanasius's childhood are unclear.

Athanasius was playing on the beach, pretending to be the apostle Peter, when Alexander invited him to be his student.

During the summer of 325, 318 bishops and pastors gathered in the ancient Greek city of Nicaea to settle the dispute regarding the divinity of Christ. Athanasius was in his late twenties at the time and accompanied Alexander as a deacon and principal secretary, although he did not formally have a vote in the council. After months of deliberation, the council affirmed the eternal divinity of Jesus, which led to exiling Arius and vindicating Alexander. However, while the Council of Nicaea clearly affirmed the divinity of Jesus (summarized in the Nicene Creed), the consensus surprisingly unraveled soon after the council, and the divinity of Christ was a contested doctrine for the next fifty years. By the mid-fourth century, Jerome quipped, "The whole world groaned and was astonished to find itself Arian."[2] So while Athanasius did not have a vote at the council of Nicaea, he would spend the rest of his life defending its orthodox doctrine, particularly the deity of Christ. For this reason, Athanasius has been lionized as the "Champion of Nicaea."

Three years after returning to Egypt, Alexander died and Athanasius, still in his early thirties, was appointed as the bishop of Alexandria. Second only to Rome, Alexandria was an extremely influential city in the ancient world. The Egyptian city (named after Greek conqueror Alexander the Great) was a cultural center in the Roman Empire, with representatives from all the major schools of philosophy and with significant contributions in the arts and sciences. Furthermore, as a trade crossroads in the Mediterranean world, Alexandria connected the Roman Empire with the markets of China, Arabia, and India. As a cosmopolitan

---

2   Jerome, "The Dialogue Against the Luciferians," 19, trans. W. H. Fremantle, in vol. 6 of *The Nicene and Post-Nicene Fathers*, Series 2, ed. Philip Schaff and Henry Wace, 14 vols., repr. ed. (Peabody, MA: Hendrickson, 1994), 329.

city, Alexandria was a melting pot of Egyptians, Greeks, Jews, and people from various other nations. As Gregory of Nazianzus once said, "The bishop of Alexandria was the bishop of the whole world."[3]

Athanasius would spend the rest of his life as the bishop of Alexandria. However, while he was unwavering in his commitment to Christ and the church, his life would be anything but stable. After seven years as bishop, a council wrongly accused Athanasius of murder and Constantine sent him into exile in Gaul (an area now located in modern Germany) in order to maintain the unity and peace of the empire. Athanasius would eventually be exiled five times, spending seventeen of his forty-six years as bishop in exile. It was there, in exile (most often in the desert), that Athanasius would do much of his writing. But while Athanasius's enemies fiercely opposed him, he was deeply loved by the church abroad and particularly by the people of Alexandria. When Athanasius would return from exile there would be parades in the streets and the people would rejoice that their bishop had returned. Athanasius was not merely a theologian; he was a pastor who loved people as much as he loved the truth.

Athanasius died in his seventies (in AD 373), having lived a long and full life. His reputation was second to none and he was praised for his virtue, passion, and theology. In his funeral oration, Gregory of Nazianzus said, "His life and conduct form the ideal of an office of pastoral leadership and his teaching the law of orthodoxy."[4] And

---

3 Peter Barnes, *Athanasius of Alexandria: His Life and Impact*, rev. ed., Early Church Fathers (Fearn, Scotland: Christian Focus, 2019), 74.

4 Khaled Anatolios, *Athanasius*, The Early Church Fathers (New York: Routledge, 2004), 33.

The Council of Nicaea began as an in-house squabble between Egyptian church leaders Pastor Arius and Bishop Alexander.

yet, Athanasius's impact goes far beyond the fourth century. His championing of Nicaea laid a foundation for Christians across the world for centuries to come. As John Behr has said, "Nicene Christianity exists by virtue of his constancy and vision."[5]

Timeline of Athanasius's Life

296	Born
318	Arian Controversy Breaks Out
324	Constantine Becomes Sole Emperor of Rome
325	Council of Nicaea
328	Becomes Bishop of Alexandria
328–335	Writes *On the Incarnation*
335–337	First Exile (Gaul)
339–346	Second Exile (Rome)
356–362	Third Exile (Egyptian Desert)
356	Writes *The Life of Antony*
362–364	Fourth Exile (Egyptian Desert)
365–366	Fifth Exile (Egyptian Desert)
373	Athanasius Dies

---

5 John Behr, "Introduction," in Saint Athanasius, *On the Incarnation*, Popular Patristics Series 44B (Yonkers, NY: St. Vladimirs Seminary Press, 2011), 19.

The Council of Nicaea affirmed the divinity of Jesus, but consensus soon unraveled. Athanasius spent much of his life defending Nicene orthodoxy.

The Theology of Athanasius

Athanasius offers a unique and rich theological contribution to the church. There are five defining characteristics of his theology.

Radically Christ-Centered

For Athanasius, Jesus is the apex of the biblical story and the center of Christian theology. While there are many different doctrines and stories in the Bible, they all find their coherence in the Son of God. To be clear, the Son is sent by the Father and empowered by the Holy Spirit—Athanasius has a deeply trinitarian theology. But the Son is central because the Father is revealed through the Son (John 1:18) and the Spirit's role is to witness to the Son (John 16:33).[6] Furthermore, Athanasius's focus is not only on the person of Christ but also the work of Christ. While Athanasius is known for defending the divinity of Jesus, he does so to show that Jesus truly is our Savior. In other words, if Jesus is not fully God and fully human, he cannot rescue humanity and renew creation.[7] For this reason, it is important when reading *On the Incarnation* to recognize that Athanasius does not use the word "incarnation" in the

---

6 A fair critique of *On the Incarnation* is that it completely leaves out the role of the Spirit. However, while this is true of Athanasius's early works, his later works clearly valued the role of the Spirit. See Athanasius, "Letters to Serapion on the Holy Spirit," in *Works on the Spirit: Athanasius and Didymus*, trans. Mark DelCogliano, Andrew Radde-Gallwitz, and Lewis Ayres, Popular Patristics Series 43 (Yonkers, NY: St. Vladimirs Seminary Press, 2011), 51–138.

7 As Thomas Weinandy says, "The whole of Athanasius's theological programme is thoroughly soteriological. Everything he teaches and upholds, every theological conflict he engages, is motivated and driven by his desire to ensure that the Christian gospel of salvation, as expressed in Scripture and as taught within the ecclesial tradition, is upheld, as well as correctly conceived and properly expressed" (*Athanasius: A Theological Introduction* [Washington, DC: Catholic University of America Press, 2018], vii).

way many Christians do today (referring to the moment of Christ taking on flesh). Rather, for Athanasius, the incarnation refers to the whole of Christ's work, including not only his assuming human nature but also his life, death, and resurrection.[8] And yet, while Athanasius wants us to see the significance of all of Christ's work, he also boldly declares that the cross is "the very center of our faith,"[9] which is why he introduces *On the Incarnation* as a defense of the cross.[10] For Athanasius, to be Christ-centered is to be cross-centered.

Framed by the Story of Scripture

While Jesus is the center of Christianity for Athanasius, Christ can only truly be understood within the whole biblical narrative that begins with creation and ends with re-creation.[11] This is especially relevant today because many contemporary Christians (especially American evangelicals) are prone to read Scripture as a two-chapter story: fall and redemption—with a gospel message that

---

8   According to Peter Leithart, "For Athanasius, 'incarnation' describes not merely the event of the Son becoming flesh but the whole life and work of Jesus" (*Athanasius*, Foundations of Theological Exegesis and Christian Spirituality [Grand Rapids: Baker Academic, 2011], 126).

9   *On the Incarnation*, §19. Anatolios notes, "The death of Christ thus occupies a central place in Athanasius's presentation of the rationale and salvific efficacy of the humanization of the Word" (*Athanasius*, 56–57).

10 See *On the Incarnation*, §1. John Behr explains, "These works are clearly, first and foremost, understood by their author to be an apology for the cross: they will show that 'he who ascended the cross is the Word of God' and that therefore the Christian faith is not 'without its word,' 'irrational' (*alogos*)" ("Introduction," 21).

11 Thomas Weinandy asserts, "The biblical narrative is Athanasius's soteriological template, beginning with the act of creation and concluding with Jesus's glorious Second Coming at the end of time" ("Athanasius's Incarnational Soteriology," in Adam J. Johnson, ed., *T&T Clark Companion to Atonement* [New York: T&T Clark, 2017], 135).

says, "We are sinners, but Christ is a Savior." While this is correct, it is not complete. The Bible is a four-chapter story—creation, fall, redemption, re-creation—of which Christ is the climax. This is why, in *On the Incarnation*, Athanasius is adamant about beginning with creation. If one does not start with creation, then it is not clear what we are saved from (sin, death, and the corruption of the world) and what we are saved for (a renewed creation with immortal resurrection bodies). When understood within the biblical narrative, salvation is not an escape from creation, but rather the restoration of creation. In Christ, God is re-creating the world by grace.

Comprehensive Salvation

Why did God become human? At the most basic level, God became human for our salvation. But while many Christians tend to reduce the work of salvation to one of its aspects (e.g., forgiveness or justification), Athanasius embraces a comprehensive understanding of the Savior's work. Athanasius certainly prioritizes particular aspects of salvation, such as the restoration of incorruptible life (2 Tim 1:10), being renewed in the image of God (Col 3:10), and participating in God's nature (2 Pet 1:4). But the Champion of Nicaea does so in a way that celebrates the many facets of salvation (e.g., victory, forgiveness, reconciliation) within the broader framework of re-creating the world through the Son. As Athanasius says, "So many are the Savior's achievements that follow from his incarnation, that to try to number them is like gazing at the open sea and trying to count the waves."[12] Because Athanasius has a holistic approach to Christ's work, he can be a unifying

---

12 *On the Incarnation*, §54.

figure for people who often divide into various camps. While Eastern Orthodox Christians love Athanasius for his emphasis on immortality and participating in the divine life, Western Christians appreciate his focus on substitutionary atonement and sacrifice. Together, we can all see how Athanasius points toward the whole Christ who accomplishes a work of holistic salvation.

Culturally Subversive

Athanasius lived and wrote as a man who was rooted in the church while also aware of his context within the world. His particular location, Alexandria, represented a global marketplace of ideas and therefore provided a stark contrast for his Christ-exalting theology. A way of summarizing Athanasius's posture toward his city and the world would be to say that he was *against the world for the sake of the world*. Athanasius was, as one of the titles of his works suggests, *contra mundum*—against the world. He acknowledged the distinction between the church and the world and called Christians to resist worldly patterns and powers that undermine God's purposes. And yet, Athanasius was not against the world in the sense that he longed to see its destruction. Rather, Athanasius opposed the world because he was ultimately for the God-designed good of the world. He longed and prayed for his city to experience the love of God in Christ. This is why, in *On the Incarnation*, after laying forth the meaning of Christ's life, death, and resurrection, Athanasius anticipates and responds to the questions and critiques from the Jews and gentiles. He subverted the ways of the world in order to seek the renewal of the world.

Aimed at Renewal

Athanasius was many things (bishop, theologian, ascetic[13]), but he was first and foremost a pastor who proclaimed truth as a way of caring for his people. He believed, as Scripture teaches, that theology is for life. In fact, the majority of Athanasius's writings are letters or essays that are responding to particular needs in the church. And just as the apostle Paul told the young Timothy to watch his doctrine and life closely (1 Tim 4:16), Athanasius concludes *On the Incarnation* by talking about how biblical truth and a godly life must go hand in hand. For Athanasius, the Christian life finds its place within the story of God's re-creation project. Just as God is renewing creation through his Son, the Christian life is one of renewal in Christ. "Therefore, if anyone is in Christ, he is a new creation. The old has gone; behold, the new has come" (2 Cor 5:17). This is why *On the Incarnation*, although primarily a book about Christ, is still a book on the Christian life. Because, for Athanasius, the Christian life is grounded in the good news of what Christ has done for us. A Christ-centered theology is the foundation for a Christ-centered life. As Peter Leithart says, "For Athanasius . . . the contemplative gaze is a transforming gaze."[14] As we fix our eyes on Jesus, understanding and experiencing the fullness of his grace, we are transformed from one degree of glory to the next. The Christian life is about being renewed into the image of Christ by the Spirit to the glory of the Father.

---

13 Ascetic – A person with an intense focus on the discipline of soul and body. The Greek root of the word is also the basis for the word "monk."

14 Leithart, *Athanasius*, 62.

The Writings of Athanasius

Athanasius was a prolific writer who left behind numerous books, treatises, and letters.[15] This volume includes *On the Incarnation* in its entirety along with portions of *The Life of Antony* and *On the Psalms*. A few words about each will help orient the reader to what lies ahead.

On the Incarnation[16]

While most of Athanasius's writings are occasional (responding to heresy, writing pastoral letters, and so on), *On the Incarnation* is his most constructive contribution. Athanasius refers to *On the Incarnation* as "a brief statement of the faith of Christ"[17]—in other words, a primer on Christianity. In short, in this book, Athanasius shows why God became human and unpacks the meaning of his death and resurrection for our salvation and for the renewal of creation. This renewal in Christ is the basis for the Christian life.

The Life of Antony

While *On the Incarnation* shows that Christ is the source of the Christian life, *The Life of Antony* gives an embodied example of the Christian life. By observing Antony, an Egyptian Christian who shaped the monastic movement[18]

---

15 Most of these are available in Athanasius, *Select Writings and Letters*, trans. Archibald Robertson, vol. 4 of *The Nicene and Post-Nicene Fathers*, Series 2, ed. Philip Schaff and Henry Wace, 14 vols., repr. ed. (Peabody, MA: Hendrickson, 2012).

16 The full title is *Treatise by the Same Author on the Incarnation of the Word and His Manifestation to Us through the Body*.

17 *On the Incarnation*, §56.

18 The Monastic Movement – The patristics-era phenomenon of many Christians radically devoting themselves to Christ through a simple life of prayer and discipline. Some of these monks sought this alone, while others

Introduction 15

in the early church, we learn that renewal in Christ comes through prayer, discipline, simplicity, spiritual warfare, and constant dependence on God.

On the Psalms

In a letter written to a man named Marcellinus, Athanasius reveals how the Scriptures (especially the Psalms) are essential for the Christian life. While all of Scripture points to Jesus, each psalm provides an invitation to experience God in a different way through a different circumstance.

Notes on the Texts and Translations

My goal in this book is to provide texts that are faithful to Athanasius's original writings while also making them readable and accessible to everyday Christians. Of the three works in this volume, none of the original editions have chapters or paragraph headings. Therefore, the chapter divisions, titles, and paragraph headings are all mine. I have also added introductions and outlines to each work, along with brief introductions at the beginning of each chapter.

For *On the Incarnation* and *The Life of Antony*, I have used the classic translations that appear in Nicene Post-Nicene Fathers and adapted the translations in the following ways:

- Updating archaic language such as "wherefore," "thither," "Godhead," and "artificer."

- Replacing British spelling with American spelling (e.g., humanisation/humanization).

---

formed communities around their common pursuit. See Greg Peters, *The Story of Monasticism: Retrieving an Ancient Tradition for Contemporary Spirituality* (Grand Rapids: Baker Academic, 2015).

- Smoothing out some awkwardly translated phrases.
- Replacing Scripture quotations with the ESV translation.
- Changing the generic "man/men" to "people" or "humanity."

All of this was done while consulting the original Greek editions and comparing them to other English translations. I have also added footnotes throughout to help the reader in areas where the text might be confusing due to a lack of background knowledge.

For *On the Psalms*, I have used a recent translation by Joel Elowsky,[19] with only two adaptations. First, I added headings to each paragraph. Second, I inserted the Scripture reference into the text in parentheses rather than in footnotes.

Outline of *On the Incarnation*

1. Creation as the Foundation of Salvation

    §1: Beginning with Creation

    §2: Competing Views of Creation

    §3: The True Doctrine of Creation

2. Human Sin and the Divine Dilemma

    §4: The Corruption of Humanity

    §5: Sin Brings Death and Destruction

---

[19] Athanasius of Alexandria, *Letter to Marcellinus on the Psalms*, trans. Joel C. Elowsky (New Haven, CT: ICCS Press, 2021).

§6: The Divine Dilemma

§7: Why Repentance Is Not Enough

3. **The Incarnation as the Divine Solution**

    §8: He Took a Body so that He Could Die

    §9: A Sufficient Exchange for All

    §10: Destroying Death and Giving Life

    §11: Misguided Worship

    §12: How God Reveals Himself

    §13: God Re-Creates Humanity in His Image through his Son

    §14: The Renewal of Humanity

    §15: Knowing God

    §16: Banishing Death, Making All Things New

    §17: In the World, yet Sustaining the Universe

    §18: Truly God, Truly Man

    §19: The Cross Reveals Christ's Divinity

4. **The Death of Christ**

    §20: He Came to Die

    §21: Could Jesus Have Died by Other Means?

    §22: Could Jesus Have Avoided Death?

    §23: What If Jesus Faked His Death?

- §24: Why Not an Honorable Death?
- §25: Why Jesus Had to Die by Crucifixion

5. **The Resurrection of Christ**
   - §26: The Resurrection as the Pledge of Christ's Victory on the Cross
   - §27: No Fear of Death
   - §28: The Conquest of Death
   - §29: Trampling Death
   - §30: Christ's Resurrection Proven through the Transformed Lives of Believers
   - §31: Christ's Resurrection Proven through His Works Today
   - §32: Christ's Resurrection Proven through His Power Manifested

6. **Refutation of the Jews**
   - §33: The Old Testament Declares Christ
   - §34: The Old Testament Foretells Christ's Death for Us
   - §35: The Old Testament Prophecies the Cross and Virgin Birth
   - §36: Jesus Is Greater than Abraham, Moses, and David
   - §37: Jesus Is the Fulfillment of the Old Testament

§38:   Jesus Is the Fulfillment of the Prophets

§39:   Jesus Is the "Anointed One" from the Book of Daniel

§40:   The Jewish Messiah Has Already Come

7. **Refutation of the Gentiles**

§41:   The Reasonableness of the Incarnation

§42:   Can Christ Pervade All Things and Be in a Body?

§43:   Why Did God Not Enter Creation as Something Else?

§44:   Could God Not Save by His Will Alone?

§45:   Christ in All of Creation

§46:   Jesus Is Greater than Idols

§47:   Jesus Is Greater than Demons

§48:   Jesus Is Greater than Magicians

§49:   Jesus Is Greater than Greek Gods

§50:   Jesus Is Greater than Kings of the Earth

§51:   Who Else Could Bring Sexual Purity and the End of Warfare?

§52:   Who Else Could Turn Enemies into Friends?

§53:   Who Else Could Accomplish So Much?

§54:   The Savior's Achievements Are More than We Could Imagine

§55: Christ Triumphs over Idolatry, Greek Wisdom, and Magic

8. **Living to the Glory of God**

§56: The First and Second Comings of Christ

§57: Christian Virtue Must Guide the Mind

The Text

Theology & Ethics

Chapter 1
Creation as the Foundation of Salvation

Athanasius seeks to explain why God became human and to show that the cross is not folly but the very wisdom of God. He begins with creation, for all was created through the Word and will be re-created through the Word. Humanity is made in the image of God for the purpose of knowing their Maker and sharing in his incorruptible life. After refuting false views of creation based on Greek philosophy, Athanasius proclaims the true doctrine of creation—that God created everything out of nothing through his Son, Jesus Christ.

***

§1 – Beginning with Creation

In our former book[1] we dealt fully enough with a few of the chief points about the pagan worship of idols, and how those

---

1   Athanasius refers to his previous book, *Against the Gentiles*. These two books—*Against the Gentiles* and *On the Incarnation*—closely relate. *Against the Gentiles*

false fears originally arose. We also, by God's grace, briefly indicated that the Word[2] of the Father is himself divine, that all things that exist owe their being to his will and power, and that it is through him that the Father gives order to creation, by him that all things are moved, and through him that they receive their being. Come now blessed one, true lover of Christ, we must take a step further in the faith of our holy religion and consider also the Word's becoming man and his divine appearing in our midst. That mystery the Jews slander, the Greeks mock, but we adore; and your own love and devotion to the Word also will be the greater, because in his humanity he seems so little worth. For it is a fact that the more unbelievers pour scorn on him, so much more does he make his divinity evident. The things which they, as people, rule out as impossible, he plainly shows to be possible; that which they mock as unfitting, his goodness makes most fit; and things which these unbelievers laugh at as "human" he by his inherent might declares divine. Thus by what seems his utter poverty and weakness on the cross he overturns the pomp and parade of idols, and quietly and hiddenly wins over the mockers and unbelievers to recognize him as God.

Now in dealing with these matters it is necessary first to recall what has already been said. You must understand why it is that the Word of the Father, so great and so high, has been made manifest in bodily form. He has not assumed a body as proper to his own nature—far from it, for as the Word he is without body. He has been

---

discusses the problems of sin and idolatry, while *On the Incarnation* focuses on the solution in Christ.

2   Athanasius commonly refers to Jesus as "the Word," drawing especially from John 1: "The Word became flesh and dwelt among us" (John 1:14).

Chapter 1: Creation as the Foundation of Salvation

manifested in a human body for this reason only, out of the love and goodness of his Father, for the salvation of us. We will begin, then, with the creation of the world and with God its Maker, for the first fact that you must grasp is this: the renewal of creation has been wrought by the self-same Word who made it in the beginning. There is thus no inconsistency between creation and salvation, for the one Father has employed the same Agent for both works, effecting the salvation of the world through the same Word who made it in the beginning.

The renewal of creation has been wrought by the self-same Word who made it in the beginning.

---

§2 – Competing Views of Creation

In regard to the making of the universe and the creation of all things there have been various opinions, and each person has propounded the theory that suited his own taste. For instance, some say that all things are self-originated and, so to speak, haphazard. The Epicureans[3] are among these; they deny that there is any Mind behind the universe at all. This view is contrary to all the facts of experience, their own existence included. For if all things had come into being in this automatic fashion, instead of being the outcome of Mind, though they existed, they would all be uniform and without distinction. In the universe everything would be sun or moon or whatever it was, and in the human body the whole would be hand

---

3 Epicureans – People who followed the teachings of the Greek philosopher Epicurus. They denied the existence of a creator and sought meaning and pleasure in the material world.

or eye or foot. But in point of fact the sun and the moon and the earth are all different things, and even within the human body there are different members, such as foot and hand and head. This distinctness of things argues not a spontaneous generation but a prevenient Cause; and from that Cause we can apprehend God, the Designer and Maker of all.

Others take the view expressed by Plato, that giant among the Greeks. He said that God had made all things out of preexistent and uncreated matter, just as the carpenter makes things only out of wood that already exists. But those who hold this view do not realize that to deny that God is himself the Cause of matter is to impute limitation to him, just as it is undoubtedly a limitation on the part of the carpenter that he can make nothing unless he has the wood. How could God be called Maker and Creator if his ability to make depended on some other cause, namely on matter itself? If he only worked up existing matter and did not himself bring matter into being, he would be not the Creator but only a craftsman.

Then, again, there is the theory of the Gnostics,[4] who have invented for themselves a Creator of all things other than the Father of our Lord Jesus Christ. These simply shut their eyes to the obvious meaning of Scripture. For instance, the Lord, having reminded the Jews of the statement in Genesis, "he who created them from the beginning made them male and female" (Matt 19:4), and having shown that for that reason a man should leave his parents and cleave to his wife, goes on to say with reference to the

---

4 Gnostics – People who made a sharp distinction between the material and spiritual realms (prioritizing the spiritual realm) and believed that salvation came through secret knowledge.

Creator, "What therefore God has joined together, let not man separate" (Matt 19:6). How can they get a creation independent of the Father out of that? And again, John, speaking all inclusively, says, "All things were made through him, and without him was not any thing made that was made" (John 1:3). How then could the Creator be someone different, other than the Father of Christ?

§3 – The True Doctrine of Creation

Such are the notions which people put forward. But the impiety of their foolish talk is plainly declared by the divine teaching of the Christian faith. From it we know that, because there is Mind behind the universe, it did not originate itself; because God is infinite, not finite, it was not made from preexistent matter, but out of nothing and out of absolute and utter nonexistence God brought it into being through the Word. He says as much in Genesis, "In the beginning, God created the heavens and the earth" (Gen 1:1), and again through that most helpful book *The Shepherd*, "Believe that there is one God who created and finished all things, and made all things out of nothing."[5] Paul also indicates the same thing when he says, "By faith we understand that the universe was created by the word of God, so that what is seen was not made out of things that are visible"(Heb 11:3). For God is good—or rather, of all goodness he is Fountainhead, and it is impossible for one who is good to be mean or grudging about anything. Grudging existence to none therefore, he made all things out of nothing through his own Word, our Lord Jesus Christ and of all these his earthly creatures he reserved

---

5 F. Crombie, trans., *The Shepherd of Hermas*, 2.1, in vol. 2 of *The Ante-Nicene Fathers*, ed. Alexander Roberts, James Donaldson, and A. Cleveland Coxe, 10 vols., repr. ed. (Peabody, MA: Hendrickson, 1994).

special mercy for the race of humanity. Upon them, therefore, upon people who, as animals, were essentially impermanent, he bestowed a grace which other creatures lacked—namely the impress of his own image, a share in the reasonable being of the very Word himself, so that, reflecting him and themselves becoming reasonable and expressing the mind of God even as he does, though in limited degree they might continue forever in the blessed and only true life of the saints in paradise. But since the will of people could turn either way, God secured this grace that he had given by making it conditional from the first upon two things—namely, a law and a place. He set them in his own paradise, and laid upon them a single prohibition. If they guarded the grace and retained the loveliness of their original innocence, then the life of paradise should be theirs, without sorrow, pain, or care, and after it the assurance of immortality in heaven. But if they went astray and became vile, throwing away their birthright of beauty, then they would come under the natural law of death and live no longer in paradise, but, dying outside of it, continue in death and in corruption. This is what Holy Scripture tells us, proclaiming the command of God, "You may surely eat of every tree of the garden, but of the tree of the knowledge of good and evil you shall not eat, for in the day that you eat of it you shall surely die" (Gen 2:16–17). *You shall surely die*—not just die only, but remain in the state of death and of corruption.

Discussion Questions

Why is it important for Athanasius to begin with creation? What might go wrong if we attempt to talk about salvation apart from the backdrop of creation?

Read John 1:1–3. Was Jesus involved with creation? If so, what role did he play?

Many contemporary Western people attempt to create their own identity and purpose. How does being created by God impact the way we view ourselves?

How does seeing every person as an image-bearer of God (and therefore equally worthy of dignity and value) impact the way we treat people?

Every gift in our lives comes from our Creator who made all things for his glory and our good. What are some gifts from God in your life that perhaps you have overlooked or taken for granted? What habits might prompt gratitude in your heart?

THEOLOGY & ETHICS

Chapter 2
Human Sin and the Divine Dilemma

While humanity is made to know God and share in his incorruptible life, we have instead turned toward evil and worshiped the creation rather than the Creator. The penalty of our sin is corruption which leads to death, and results in destruction on a mass scale. Humanity's spoiling of God's good creation brings about a divine dilemma. On the one hand, God must be true to his word and punish sin with the penalty of death. But, on the other hand, it would be unfitting for God's good and beloved creation to merely perish. What is the solution? One thing is clear: repentance from humanity will not suffice, for it would only deal with a symptom of the problem (wrong behavior) as opposed its source (the corrupted nature of humanity). The solution must come from God.

***

§4 – The Corruption of Humanity

You may be wondering why we are discussing the origin of humanity when we set out to talk about the Word's becoming human. The former subject is relevant to the latter for this reason: it was our sorry case that caused the Word to come down, our transgression that called out his love for us, so that he made haste to help us and to appear among us. It is we who were the cause of his taking human form, and for our salvation that in his great love he was both born and manifested in a human body. For God had made people thus (that is, as embodied spirits), and had willed that they should remain in incorruption. But humanity, having turned from the contemplation of God to evil of their own devising, had come inevitably under the law of death. Instead of remaining in the state in which God had created them, they were in process of becoming corrupted entirely, and death had them completely under its dominion. For the transgression of the commandment was making them turn back again according to their nature; and as they had at the beginning come into being out of nonexistence, so were they now on the way to returning, through corruption, to nonexistence again. The presence and love of the Word had called them into being; inevitably, therefore when they lost the knowledge of God, they lost existence with it; for it is God alone who exists—evil is nonbeing, the negation and antithesis of good. By nature, of course, people are mortal, since they were made from nothing; but they bear also the likeness of him who is, and if they preserve that likeness through constant contemplation, then their nature is deprived of its power and they remain incorrupt. So is it affirmed in Wisdom: "To observe his laws is the basis for incorruptibility."[1] And being incorrupt, they would be henceforth as God, as Holy Scripture says, "I said, 'You are gods, sons of the Most High, all of you; nevertheless, like men you shall die, and fall like any prince'" (Ps 82:6–7).

§5 – Sin Brings Death and Destruction

This, then, was the plight of humanity. God had not only made them out of nothing, but had also graciously bestowed on them his own life by the grace of the Word. Then, turning from eternal things to things corruptible, by counsel of the devil, they had become the cause of their own corruption in death; for, as I said before, though they were by nature subject to corruption, the grace of their union with the Word made them capable of escaping from the natural law, provided that they retained the beauty of innocence with which they were created. That is to say, the presence of the Word with them shielded them even from natural corruption, as also Wisdom says: "God created man for incorruption and as an image of his own eternity; but by envy of the devil death entered into the world."[2] When this happened, people began to die, and corruption ran riot among them and held sway over them to an even more than natural degree, because it was the penalty of which God had forewarned them for transgressing the commandment. Indeed, they had in their sinning surpassed all limits; for, having invented wickedness in the beginning and so involved themselves in death and corruption, they had gone on gradually from bad to worse, not stopping at any one kind of evil, but continually, as with insatiable

---

1   Wis 6:18. See Robert F. Lay, ed., *Books Jesus Read: Learning from the Apocrypha*, Sacred Roots Spiritual Classics 5 (Upland, IN: Samuel Morris Publications, 2022).

2   Wis 2:23–24.

appetite, devising new kinds of sins. Adulteries and thefts were everywhere, murder and raping filled the earth, law was disregarded in corruption and injustice, all kinds of iniquities were perpetrated by all, both individually and in common. Cities were warring with cities, nations were rising against nations, and the whole earth was torn apart with factions and battles, while each strove to outdo the other in wickedness. Even crimes contrary to nature were not unknown, but as the martyr-apostle of Christ says: "Their women exchanged natural relations for those that are contrary to nature; and the men likewise gave up natural relations with women and were consumed with passion for one another, men committing shameless acts with men and receiving in themselves the due penalty for their error" (Rom 1:26–27).

It would, of course, have been unthinkable that God should go back upon his word and that humanity, having transgressed, should not die; but it was equally monstrous that beings which once had shared the nature of the Word should perish and turn back again into nonexistence through corruption.

---

§6 – The Divine Dilemma

We saw in the last section that because death and corruption were gaining ever firmer hold on them, the human race was in the process of destruction. People, who were created in God's image and in their possession of reason reflected the very Word himself, were disappearing, and the work of God was being undone. The law of death, which followed from the transgression, prevailed upon us, and from it there was no escape. The thing that was happening was in truth both monstrous and unfitting. It would, of course, have been unthinkable that God should go back upon his word and that humanity, having transgressed, should not die; but it was equally monstrous that beings which once had shared the nature of the Word should perish and turn back again into nonexistence through corruption. It was unworthy of the goodness of God that creatures made by him should be brought to nothing through the deceit wrought upon humanity by the devil; and it was supremely unfitting that the work of God in mankind should disappear, either through their own negligence or through the deceit of evil spirits. As, then, the creatures whom he had created reasonable, like the Word, were in fact perishing, and such noble works were on the road to ruin, what then was God, being good, to do? Was he to let corruption and death have their way with them? In that case, what was the use of having made them in the beginning? Surely it would have been better never to have been created at all than, having been created, to be neglected and perish; and, besides that, such indifference to the ruin of his own work before his very eyes would argue not goodness in God but limitation, and that far more than if he had never created people at all. It was impossible, therefore, that God should leave humanity to be carried off by corruption, because it would be unfitting and unworthy of himself.

§7 – Why Repentance Is Not Enough

Yet, true though this is, it is not the whole matter. As we have already noted, it was unthinkable that God, the Father of Truth, should go back upon his word regarding death in order to ensure our continued existence. He could not falsify himself: what, then, was God to do? Was he to demand repentance from men for their transgression? You might say that that was worthy of God, and argue further that, as through the transgression they became subject to corruption, so through repentance they might return to incorruption again. But repentance would not guard the divine consistency, for, if death did not hold dominion over humanity, God would still remain untrue.

For he alone, being Word of the Father and above all, was in consequence both able to re-create all, and worthy to suffer on behalf of all and to be an ambassador for all with the Father.

Nor does repentance recall people from what is according to their nature; all that it does is make them cease from sinning. Had it been a case of a trespass only, and not of a subsequent corruption, repentance would have been well enough; but once transgression had begun humanity came under the power of the corruption proper to their nature and were bereft of the grace which belonged to them as creatures in the image of God. No, repentance could not meet the case. What—or rather, who—was it that was needed for such grace and such recall as we required? Who, save the Word of God himself, who also in the beginning had made all things out of nothing? His part it was, and his alone, both to bring again the corruptible to incorruption and to maintain for the Father his consistency of character with all. For he alone, being Word of the Father and above all, was in consequence both able to re-create all, and worthy to suffer on behalf of all and to be an ambassador for all with the Father.

Discussion Questions

 In §5, Athanasius describes the widespread effects of sin that he sees in the world. How do you see the effects of sin in our world today?

 Can you summarize "God's dilemma" in your own words?

 Why is repentance not enough to deal with the problem of sin?

 How can you practically show God's love to someone this week who is suffering under the effects of our fallen world?

 Read 1 John 1:9. Do you have regular rhythms of confession in your life? If so, how has that shaped you over time? If not, will you consider implementing such rhythms?

THEOLOGY & ETHICS

Chapter 3
The Incarnation as the Divine Solution

How can God uphold his purposes for his beloved creation while also dealing with sin, corruption, and death? God's solution is to send his Son in the flesh to re-create the world by grace. Jesus, who by nature could not die, took on a human body so that he might die in place of sinners, thereby abolishing death and giving new life. While humanity has rejected God and worshiped creation instead of the Creator, the good news of Jesus restores our relationship with God and redirects our worship back to him. God's solution to the dilemma is to send his Son as man in order to destroy death, renew humanity in the image of God, and re-create the world through the counterintuitive means of crucifixion.

***

§8 – He Took a Body so that He Could Die

For this purpose, then, the incorporeal, incorruptible, and immaterial Word of God entered our world. In one sense, indeed, he was not far from it before, for no part of creation had ever been without him who, while ever abiding in union with the Father, yet fills all things that are. But now he entered the world in a new way, stooping to our level in his love and self-revealing to us. He saw the reasonable race, the race of humanity that, like himself, expressed the Father's mind, wasting out of existence, and death reigning over all in corruption. He saw that corruption held us all the closer, because it was the penalty for the transgression; he saw, too, how unthinkable it would be for the law to be repealed before it was fulfilled. He saw how unfitting it was that the very things of which he himself was the Creator should be disappearing. He saw how the surpassing wickedness of humanity was mounting up against them; he saw also their universal liability to death. All this he saw and—pitying our race, moved with compassion for our limitation, unable to endure that death should have the mastery—rather than that his creatures should perish and the work of his Father for us come to nothing, he took to himself a body, a human body even as our own. Nor did he will merely to become embodied or merely to appear; had that been so, he could have revealed his divine majesty in some other and better way. No, he took our body, and not only so, but he took it directly from a spotless, stainless virgin, without the agency of human father—a pure body, untainted by intercourse with man. He, the Mighty One, the Creator of all, himself prepared this body in the Virgin as a temple for himself, and took it for his very own, as the instrument through which he was known and in which he dwelt. Thus, taking a body like our own, because all our bodies were liable to the corruption of death, he surrendered his body to death instead of all, and offered it to the Father. This he did out of sheer love for us, so that

Chapter 3: The Incarnation as the Divine Solution   41

He prepared this body in the Virgin as temple for himself.

in his death all might die, and the law of death thereby be abolished because, having fulfilled in his body that for which it was appointed, it was thereafter voided of its power for humanity. This he did that he might turn again to incorruption people who had turned back to corruption, and make them alive through death by the appropriation of his body and by the grace of his resurrection. Thus he would make death to disappear from them as utterly as straw from fire.

He assumed a body capable of death, in order that it, through belonging to the Word who is above all, might become in dying a sufficient exchange for all

---

§9 – A Sufficient Exchange for All

The Word perceived that corruption could not be got rid of otherwise than through death; yet he himself, as the Word, being immortal and the Father's Son, was such as could not die. For this reason, therefore, he assumed a body capable of death, in order that it, through belonging to the Word who is above all, might become in dying a sufficient exchange for all, and, itself remaining incorruptible through his indwelling, might thereafter put an end to corruption for all others as well, by the grace of the resurrection. It was by surrendering to death the body which he had taken, as an offering and sacrifice free from every stain, that he at once abolished death for his human brothers and sisters by the offering of the equivalent. For naturally, since the Word of God was above all, when he offered his own temple and bodily instrument as a substitute for the life of all, he fulfilled in death all that was required. Naturally also, through this union of the immortal Son of God with our human nature, all people were clothed with incorruption in the promise of the resurrection. For the solidarity of mankind is such that, by virtue of the Word's indwelling in a single human body, the corruption which goes with death has lost its power over all. You know how it is when some great king enters a large city and dwells in one of its houses; because of his dwelling in that single house, the whole city is honored, and enemies and robbers cease to harass it. Even so is it with the King of all; he has come into our country and dwelt in one body amidst the many, and in consequence the designs of the enemy against mankind have been foiled and the corruption of death, which formerly held them in its power, has simply ceased to be. For the human race would have perished utterly had not the Lord and Savior of all, the Son of God, come among us to put an end to death.

§10 – Destroying Death and Giving Life

This great work was, indeed, supremely worthy of the goodness of God. A king who has founded a city, so far from neglecting it when through the carelessness of the inhabitants it is attacked by robbers, avenges it and saves it from destruction, having regard rather to his own honor than to the people's neglect. Much more, then, the Word of the all-good Father was not unmindful of the human race that he had called to be; but rather, by the offering of his own body he abolished the death which they had incurred, and corrected their neglect by his own teaching. Thus by his own power he restored the whole nature of humanity. The Savior's own inspired disciples assure us of this. We read in one place: "For the love of Christ controls us, because we have concluded this: that one has died for all, therefore all have died; and he died for all, that those who live might no longer live for themselves but for him who for their sake died and was raised" (2 Cor 5:14–15). And again another says: "But we see him who for a little while was made lower than the angels, namely Jesus, crowned with glory and honor because of the suffering of death, so that by the grace of God he might taste death for everyone" (Heb 2:9). The same writer goes on to point out why it was necessary for God the Word and none other to become man: "For it was fitting that he, for whom and by whom all things exist, in bringing many sons to glory, should make the founder of their salvation perfect through suffering" (Heb 2:10). He means that the rescue of mankind from corruption was the proper part only of him who made them in the beginning. He points out also that the Word assumed a human body, expressly in order that he might offer it in sacrifice for other like bodies: "Since therefore the children share in flesh and blood, he himself likewise partook of the same things, that through death he might destroy the one who has the power of death, that is, the devil" (Heb 2:14). For by the sacrifice of his own body he did two things: he put an end to the law of death which barred our way, and he made a new beginning of life for us, by giving us the hope of resurrection. By man death has gained its power over men; by the Word made man death has been destroyed and life raised up anew. That is what Paul says, that true servant of Christ: "For as by a man came death, by a man has come also the resurrection of the dead. For as in Adam all die, so also in Christ shall all be made alive" (1 Cor 15:21–22), and so forth. Now, therefore, when we die we no longer do so as people condemned to death. But as those who are even now in the process of rising, we await the general resurrection of all, "which he will display at the proper time" (1 Tim 6:15), even God who wrought it and bestowed it on us.

> *The Word assumed a human body, expressly in order that he might offer it in sacrifice for other like bodies.*

This, then, is the first cause of the Savior's becoming human. There are, however, other things which show how wholly fitting is his blessed presence in our midst; and these we must now go on to consider.

§11 – Misguided Worship

When God the Almighty was making humankind through his own Word, he perceived that they, owing to the limitation of their nature, could not of themselves have any knowledge of their Creator, the Incorporeal and Uncreated. He took pity on them, therefore, and did not leave them destitute of the knowledge of himself, lest their very existence should prove purposeless. For of what use is existence to the creature if it cannot know its Maker? How could men be reasonable beings if they had no knowledge of the Word and Reason of the Father, through whom they had received their being? They would be no better than the beasts, had they no knowledge save of earthly things; and why should God have made them at all if he had not intended them to know him? But, in fact, the good God has given them a share in his own Image, that is, in our Lord Jesus Christ, and has made even themselves after the same Image and Likeness. Why? Simply in order that through this gift of godlikeness in themselves they may be able to perceive the Image Absolute, that is the Word himself, and through him to apprehend the Father, knowledge of their Maker being for humanity the only really happy and blessed life.

But, as we have already seen, people, foolish as they are, thought little of the grace they had received, and turned away from God. They defiled their own soul so completely that they not only lost their apprehension of God, but invented for themselves other gods of various kinds. They fashioned idols for themselves in place of the truth and reverenced things that are not rather than God who is, worshiping "the creature rather than the Creator" (Rom 1:25). Moreover, and much worse, they transferred the honor which is due to God to material objects such as wood and stone, and also to humans; and further even than that they went, as we said in our former book. Indeed, so impious were they that they worshiped evil spirits as gods in satisfaction of their lusts. They sacrificed brute beasts and burnt people alive, as the just due of these deities, thereby bringing themselves more and more under their insane control. Magic arts also were taught among them, oracles in various places led people astray, and the cause of everything in human life was traced to the stars as though nothing existed but that which could be seen. In a word, impiety and lawlessness were everywhere, and neither God nor his Word was known. Yet he had not hidden himself from the sight of humanity nor given the knowledge of himself in one way only; but rather he had unfolded it in many forms and by many ways.

§12 – How God Reveals Himself

God knew the limitation of humankind, you see; and though the grace of being made in his image was sufficient to give them knowledge of the Word and through him of the Father, as a safeguard against their neglect of this grace, he provided the works of creation also as means by which the Maker might be known. Nor was this all. Humanity's neglect of the indwelling grace tends ever to increase; and against this further frailty also God made provision by giving them a law, and by sending prophets, people whom they knew. Thus, if they were tardy in looking up to heaven, they might still gain knowledge of their Maker from those close at hand; for people can learn directly about higher things from other people. Three ways thus lay open to them, by which they might obtain the knowledge of God. They could look up into the immensity of heaven, and by pondering the harmony of creation come to know its Ruler, the Word of the Father, whose all-ruling providence makes known the Father to all. Or, if this was beyond them, they could converse with holy people, and through them learn to know God, the Creator of all things, the Father of Christ, and to recognize the worship of idols as the negation of the truth and full of all impiety. Or else, in the third place, they could cease from lukewarmness and lead a good life merely by knowing the law. For the law was not given only for the Jews, nor was it solely for their sake that God sent the prophets, though it was to the Jews that they were sent and by the Jews that they were persecuted. The law and the prophets were a sacred school of the knowledge of God and the conduct of the spiritual life for the whole world.

So great, indeed, were the goodness and the love of God. Yet humanity, bowed down by the pleasures of the moment and by the frauds and illusions of the evil spirits, did not lift up their heads toward the truth. So burdened were they with their wickedness that they seemed rather to be brute beasts than reasonable people, reflecting the very likeness of the Word.

§13 – God Re-Creates Humanity in His Image through His Son

What was God to do in face of this dehumanizing of persons, this universal hiding of the knowledge of himself by the schemes of evil spirits? Was he to keep silence before so great a wrong and let people go on being thus deceived and kept in ignorance of himself? If so, what was the use of having made them in his own image originally? It would surely have been better for them always to have been brutes, rather than to revert to that condition when once they had shared the nature of the Word. Again, things being as they were, what was the use of their ever having had the knowledge of God? Surely it would have been better for God never to have bestowed it, than that humans should subsequently be found unworthy to receive it. Similarly, what possible profit could it be to God himself, who made humans, if when made they did not worship him, but regarded others as their makers? This would be tantamount to his having made them for others and not for himself. Even an earthly king, though he is only a man, does not allow lands that he has colonized to pass into other hands or to desert to other rulers, but sends letters and friends and even visits them himself to recall them to their allegiance, rather than allow his work to be undone. How much more, then, will God be patient and painstaking with his creatures, that they be not led astray from him to the service of those that are not, and that all the more because such error means for them sheer ruin, and because it is not right that those who had once shared his image should be destroyed.

Chapter 3: The Incarnation as the Divine Solution

> *It was he alone, the Image of the Father who could re-create humanity made after the image.*

What, then, was God to do? What else could he possibly do, being God, but renew his image in humanity, so that through it people might once more come to know him? And how could this be done except by the coming of the very image himself, our Savior Jesus Christ? Humanity could not have done it, for they are only made after the image; nor could angels have done it, for they are not the images of God. The Word of God came in his own Person, because it was he alone, the Image of the Father who could re-create humanity made after the image.

> *He assumed a human body, in order that in it death might once for all be destroyed, and that humanity might be renewed according to the image.*

In order to effect this re-creation, however, he had first to do away with death and corruption. Therefore he assumed a human body, in order that in it death might once for all be destroyed, and that humanity might be renewed according to the Image. The Image of the Father only was sufficient for this need. Here is an illustration to prove it.

§14 – The Renewal of Humanity

You know what happens when a portrait that has been painted on a panel becomes obliterated through external stains. The artist does not throw away the panel, but the subject of the portrait has to come and sit for it again, and then the likeness is redrawn on the same material. Even so was it with the all-holy Son of God. He, the Image of the Father, came and dwelt in our midst, in order that he might renew humankind made after himself, and seek out his lost sheep, even as he says in the Gospel: "For the Son of Man came to seek and to save the lost" (Luke 19:10). This also explains his saying to the Jews: "unless one is born again" (John 3:3). He was not referring to one's natural birth from his mother, as they thought, but to the rebirth and re-creation of the soul in the image of God.

He, the Image of the Father, came and dwelt in our midst, in order that he might renew humankind

---

Nor was this the only thing which only the Word could do. When the madness of idolatry and irreligion filled the world and the knowledge of God was hidden, whose part was it to teach the world about the Father? Humanity's, would you say? But people cannot run everywhere over the world, nor would their words carry sufficient weight if they did, nor would they be, unaided, a match for the evil spirits. Moreover, since even the best of people were confused and blinded by evil, how could they convert the souls and minds of others? You cannot put straight in others what is warped in yourself. Perhaps you will say, then, that creation was enough to teach people about the Father. But if that had been so, such great evils would never have occurred. Creation was there all the time, but it did not prevent people from wallowing in error. Once more, then, it was the Word of God, who sees all that is in people and moves all things in creation, who alone could meet the needs of the situation. It was his part and his alone, whose ordering of the universe reveals the Father, to renew the same teaching. But how was he to do it? By the same means as before, perhaps you will say, that is, through the works of creation. But this was proven insufficient. Humanity had neglected to consider the heavens before, and now they were looking in the opposite direction. Therefore, in all naturalness and fitness, desiring to do good to humanity, as man he dwells, taking to himself a body like the rest; and through his actions done in that body, as it were on their own level, he teaches those who would not learn by other means to know himself, the Word of God, and through him the Father.

You cannot put straight in others what is warped in yourself.

---

§15 – Knowing God

He deals with them as a good teacher with his pupils, coming down to their level and using simple means. Paul says as much: "For since, in the wisdom of God, the world did not know God through wisdom, it pleased God through the folly of what we preach to save those who believe" (1 Cor 1:21). Humanity had turned from the contemplation of God above, and were looking for him in the opposite direction, down among created things and things of sense. The Savior of us all, the Word of God, in his great love took to himself a body and moved as man among humanity, meeting their senses, so to speak, halfway. He became himself an object for the senses, so that those who were seeking God in sensible things might apprehend the Father through the works which he, the Word of God, did in the body. Human and human-minded as people were, therefore, to whichever side they looked in the sensible world they found themselves taught the truth. Were they awestruck by creation? They beheld it confessing Christ as Lord. Did their minds tend to regard people as gods? The uniqueness of the Savior's works marked him, alone of humanity, as Son of God. Were they drawn to evil spirits? They saw them driven out by the Lord and learned that the Word of God alone was God and that the evil spirits were not gods at all. Were they inclined to hero worship and the cult of the dead? Then the fact that the Savior had risen from the dead showed them how false these other deities were, and that the Word of the Father is the one true Lord, the Lord even of death. For this reason was he both born and manifested as man, for this he died and rose, in order that, eclipsing by his works all other human deeds, he might recall people from all the paths of error to know the Father. As he says himself, "For the Son of Man came to seek and to save the lost" (Luke 19:10).

§16 – Banishing Death, Making All Things New

When then, the minds of people had fallen finally to the level of sensible things, the Word submitted to appear in a body, in order that he, as man, might center their senses on himself, and convince them through his human acts that he himself is not man only but also God, the Word and Wisdom of the true God. This is what Paul wants to tell us when he says: "so that Christ may dwell in your hearts through faith—that you, being rooted and grounded in love, may have strength to comprehend with all the saints what is the breadth and length and height and depth, and to know the love of Christ that surpasses knowledge, that you may be filled with all the fullness of God" (Eph 3:17–19). The self-revealing of the Word is in every dimension—above, in creation; below, in the incarnation; in the depth, in Hades;

Chapter 3: The Incarnation as the Divine Solution

in the breadth, throughout the world. All things have been filled with the knowledge of God.

There were thus two things which the Savior did for us by becoming human. He banished death from us and made us anew.

For this reason he did not offer the sacrifice on behalf of all immediately when he came, for if he had surrendered his body to death and then raised it again at once he would have ceased to be an object of our senses. Instead of that, he stayed in his body and let himself be seen in it, doing acts and giving signs which showed him to be not only human, but also God the Word. There were thus two things which the Savior did for us by becoming human. He banished death from us and made us anew; and, invisible and imperceptible as in himself he is, he became visible through his works and revealed himself as the Word of the Father, the Ruler and King of the whole creation.

§17 – In the World, yet Sustaining the Universe

There is a paradox in this last statement which we must now examine. The Word was not hedged in by his body, nor did his presence in the body prevent his being present elsewhere as well. When he moved his body, he did not cease also to direct the universe by his mind and might. No. The marvelous truth is, that being the Word, so far from being himself contained by anything, he actually contained all things himself. In creation he is present everywhere, yet is distinct in being from it; ordering, directing, giving life to all, containing all, yet is he himself the Uncontained, existing solely in his Father. As with the whole, so also is it with the part. Existing in a human body, to which he himself gives life, he is still Source of life to all the universe, present in every part of it, yet outside the whole; and he is revealed both through the works of his body and through his activity in the world. It is, indeed, the function of a soul to behold things that are outside the body, but it cannot energize or move them. A person cannot transport things from one place to another, for instance, merely by thinking about them; nor can you or I move the sun and the stars just by sitting at home and looking at them. With the Word of God in his human nature, however, it was otherwise. His body was for him not a limitation, but an instrument, so that he was both in it and in all things, and outside all things, resting in the Father alone. At one and the same time—this is the wonder—as a man he was living a human life, and as Word he was sustaining the life of the universe, and as Son he was in constant union with the Father. Not even his birth from a virgin, therefore, changed him in any way, nor was he defiled by being in the body. Rather, he sanctified the body by being in it. For his being in everything does not mean that he shares the nature of everything, only that he gives all things their being and sustains them in it. Just as the sun is not defiled by the contact of its rays with earthly objects, but rather enlightens and purifies them, so he who made the sun is not defiled by being made known in a body, but rather the body is cleansed and quickened by his indwelling, "He committed no sin, neither was deceit found in his mouth" (1 Pet 2:22).

§18 – Truly God, Truly Man

You must understand, therefore, that when writers on this sacred theme speak of him as eating and drinking and being born, they mean that the body, as a body, was born and sustained with the food proper to its nature; while God the Word, who was united with it, was at the same time ordering the universe and revealing himself through his bodily acts as not a man only but as God. Those acts are rightly said to be his acts, because the body which did them did indeed belong to him and none other; moreover, it was right that they should be thus attributed to him as human, in order to show that his body was a real one and not merely an appearance. From such ordinary acts as being born and taking food, he was recognized as being actually present in the body; but by the extraordinary acts which he did through the body he proved himself to be the Son of God. That is the meaning of his words to the unbelieving Jews: "If I am not doing the works of my Father, then do not believe me; but if I do them, even though you do not believe me, believe the works, that you may know and understand that the Father is in me and I am in the Father" (John 10:37–38).

Invisible in himself, he is known from the works of creation; so also, when his divinity is veiled in human nature, his bodily acts still declare him to be not a man only, but the Power and Word of God. To speak authoritatively to evil spirits, for instance, and to drive them out, is not human but divine; and who could see him curing all the diseases to which humanity is prone, and still deem him mere human and not also God? He cleansed lepers, he made the lame to walk, he opened the ears of the deaf and the eyes of the blind, there was no sickness or weakness that he did not drive away. Even the most casual observer can see that these were acts of God. Consider the healing of the man born blind, for instance: who but the Father and Creator of man, the Controller of his whole being, could thus have restored the faculty denied at birth? He who did thus must surely be himself the Lord of birth. This is proved also at the outset of his becoming human. He formed his own body from the virgin; and that is no small proof of his divinity, since he who made that was the Maker of all else. And would not anyone infer from the fact of that body being begotten of a virgin only, without human father, that he who appeared in it was also the Maker and Lord of all beside?

Again, consider the miracle at Cana. Would not anyone who saw the substance of water turned into wine understand that he who did it was the Lord and Maker of the water that he changed (John 2:1–11)? It was for the same reason that he walked on the sea as on dry land—to prove to the onlookers that he had mastery over all. And the feeding of the multitude, when he made little into much, so that from five loaves five thousand mouths were filled—did not that prove him none other than the very Lord whose mind is over all?

§19 – The Cross Reveals Christ's Divinity

All these things the Savior thought fit to do, so that, recognizing his bodily acts as works of God, people who were blind to his presence in creation might regain knowledge of the Father. For, as I said before, who that saw his authority over evil spirits and their response to it could doubt that he was, indeed, the Son, the Wisdom, and the Power of God? Even the very creation broke silence at his command and, marvelous to relate, confessed with one voice before the cross, that monument of victory, that he who suffered in the body was not human only, but Son of God and Savior of all. The sun veiled its face, the earth quaked, the mountains were rent asunder, all people were stricken with awe. These things showed that Christ on the cross was God, and that all creation was his slave and was bearing witness by its fear to the presence of its Master.

Thus, then, God the Word revealed himself to humanity through his works. We must next consider the end of his earthly life and the nature of his bodily death. This is, indeed, the very center of our faith, and everywhere you hear men speak of it; by it, too, no less than by his other acts, Christ is revealed as God and Son of God.

Discussion Questions

 For Athanasius, salvation is aimed at not only human souls but also all of creation. Is that different than what you have heard in church? If so, how?

 According to Athanasius, why did God become human? Try to summarize his argument in your own words. What do you think it means to be remade into the image of God?

 If our sinful nature leads us to worship created things rather than the Creator, what is something in your life that you are tempted to value over God? What would it look like for you to allow Jesus to redirect your worship back to God?

 If God is renewing all of creation, how can you practically participate in his work of renewal in your sphere of influence? What is broken around you that you long to see made new by grace?

 Is there a Scripture you could memorize or meditate on that would help hide the truth of this chapter in your heart?

Chapter 4
The Death of Christ

According to Athanasius, Jesus came to die. As the eternal Word who was incapable of death, Jesus took on a body so that he could offer it up as a sacrifice on behalf of sinful people. And as the divine author of life, when Jesus entered into death, he annulled its power, thereby conquering the grave and re-creating incorruptible life. Athanasius entertains why Jesus could not have died by other means, or even faked his death or avoided death altogether. Rather, Jesus had to die by crucifixion. Only through crucifixion would Jesus die extending his hands to Jews and gentiles. Only through crucifixion was Jesus exalted to clear the air of the evil powers (Eph 2:2; John 12:32). The cross is the divine means of salvation.

***

§20 – He Came to Die

We have dealt as far as circumstances and our own understanding permit with the reason for his bodily manifestation. We have seen that to change the corruptible to incorruption was proper to none other than the Savior himself, who in the beginning made all things out of nothing; that only the Image of the Father could re-create the likeness of the Image in humanity, that none except our Lord Jesus Christ could give to mortals immortality, and that only the Word who orders all things and is alone the Father's true and only begotten Son (John 3:16) could teach humanity about him and abolish the worship of idols. But beyond all this, there was a debt owed which must be paid; for, as I said before, all people were due to die. Here, then, is the second reason why the Word dwelt among us, namely that having proved his divinity by his works, he might offer the sacrifice on behalf of all, surrendering his own temple to death in place of all, to settle humanity's account with death and free them from the primal transgression. In the same act also he showed himself mightier than death, displaying his own body incorruptible as the firstfruits of the resurrection.

You must not be surprised if we repeat ourselves in dealing with this subject. We are speaking of the good pleasure of God and of the things which he in his loving wisdom thought fit to do, and it is better to put the same thing in several ways than to run the risk of leaving something out. The body of the Word, then, being a real human body, in spite of its having been uniquely formed from a virgin, was of itself mortal and, like other bodies, liable to death. But the indwelling of the Word loosed it from this natural liability, so that corruption could not touch it. Thus it happened that two opposite marvels took place at once: the death of all was consummated in the Lord's body; yet, because the Word was in it, death and corruption were in the same act utterly abolished. Death there had to be, and death for all, so that the due of all might be paid. Therefore, the Word, as I said, being himself incapable of death, assumed a mortal body, that he might offer it as his own in place of all, and suffering for the sake of all through his union with it, "he might destroy the one who has the power of death, that is, the devil, and deliver all those who through fear of death were subject to lifelong slavery" (Heb 2:14–15).

§21 – Could Jesus Have Died by Other Means?

Have no fears, then. Now that the common Savior of all has died on our behalf, we who believe in Christ no longer die, as people died previously, in fulfillment of the threat of the law. That condemnation has come to an end; and now that, by the grace of the resurrection, corruption has been banished and done away, we are loosed from our mortal bodies in God's good time for each, so that we may obtain thereby a better resurrection. Like seeds cast into the earth, we do not perish in our dissolution, but like them shall rise again, death having been brought to nothing by the grace of the Savior. That is why blessed Paul, through whom we all have surety of the resurrection, says: "For this perishable body must put on the imperishable, and this mortal body must put on immortality. When the perishable puts on the imperishable, and the mortal puts on immortality, then shall come to pass the saying that is written: 'Death is swallowed up in victory.' 'O death, where is your victory? O death, where is your sting?'" (1 Cor 15:53–55).

"Well then," some people may say, "if the essential thing was that he should surrender his body to death in place of all, why did he not do so as a man privately, without going to the length of public crucifixion? Surely it would have been more suitable for him to have laid aside his body with honor than to endure so shameful a death." But look at this argument closely, and see how merely human it is, whereas what the Savior did was truly divine and worthy of his divinity for several reasons. The first is this. The death of people under ordinary circumstances is the result of their natural weakness. They are essentially impermanent, so after a time they fall ill and when worn out they die. But the Lord is not like that. He is not weak; he is the Power of God and Word of God and very Life itself. If he had died quietly in his bed like other people it would have looked as if he did so in accordance with his nature, and as though he was indeed no more than other people. But because he was himself Word, Life, and Power, his body was made strong, and because the death had to be accomplished, he took the occasion of perfecting his sacrifice not from himself, but from others. How could he fall sick, who had healed others? Or how could that body weaken and fail by means of which others are made strong? Here, again, you may say, "Why did he not prevent death, as he did sickness?" Because it was precisely in order to be able to die that he had taken a body, and to prevent the death would have been to impede the resurrection. And as to the unsuitability of sickness for his body, as arguing weakness, you may say, "Did he then not hunger?" Yes, he hungered, because that was the property of his body, but he did not die of hunger because he whose body hungered was the Lord. Similarly, though he died to ransom all, he did not see corruption. His body rose in perfect soundness, for it was the body of none other than the Life himself.

§22 – Could Jesus Have Avoided Death?

Someone else might say, perhaps, that it would have been better for the Lord to have avoided the designs of the Jews against him, and so to have guarded his body from death altogether. But see how unfitting this also would have been for him. Just as it would not have been fitting for him to give his body to death by his own hand, being Word and being Life, so also it was not consonant with himself that he should avoid the death inflicted by others. Rather, he pursued it to the uttermost, and in pursuance of his nature neither laid aside his body of his own accord nor escaped the plotting Jews. And this action showed no limitation or weakness in the Word; for he both waited for death in order to make an end of it, and hastened to accomplish it as an offering on behalf of all. Moreover, as it was the death of all mankind that the Savior came to accomplish, not his own, he did not lay aside his body by an individual act of dying, for to him, as Life, this simply did not belong; but he accepted death at the hands of people, thereby completely to destroy it in his own body.

There are some further considerations which enable one to understand why the Lord's body had such an end. The supreme object of his coming was to bring about the resurrection of the body. This was to be the monument to his victory over death, the assurance to all that he had himself conquered corruption and that their own bodies also would eventually be incorrupt; and it was in token of that and as a pledge of the future resurrection that he kept his body incorrupt. But there again, if his body had fallen sick and the Word had left it in that condition, how unfitting it would have been! Should he who healed the bodies of others neglect to keep his own in health? How would his miracles of healing be believed, if this were so? Surely people would either laugh at him as unable to dispel disease or else consider him lacking in proper human feeling because he could do so, but did not.

§23 – What If Jesus Faked His Death?

Then, again, suppose without any illness he had just concealed his body somewhere, and then suddenly reappeared and said that he had risen from the dead. He would have been regarded merely as a teller of tales, and because there was no witness of his death, nobody would believe his resurrection. Death had to precede resurrection, for there could be no resurrection without it. A secret and unwitnessed death would have left the resurrection without any proof or evidence to support it. Again, why should he die a secret death, when he proclaimed the fact of his rising openly? Why should he drive out evil spirits and heal the man blind from birth and change water into wine, all publicly, in order to convince people that he was the Word, and not also declare publicly that incorruptibility of his mortal body, so that he might himself be believed to be the Life? And how could his disciples have had boldness in speaking of the resurrection, unless they could state it as a fact that he had first died? Or how could their hearers be expected to believe their assertion, unless they themselves also had witnessed his death? For if the Pharisees at the time refused to believe and forced others to deny also, though the things had happened before their very eyes, how many excuses for unbelief would they have contrived if it had taken place secretly? Or how could the end of death and the victory over it have been declared, had not the Lord thus challenged it before the sight of all and by the incorruption of his body proved that from now on it was annulled and void?

§24 – Why Not an Honorable Death?

There are some other possible objections that must be answered. Some might urge that, even granting the necessity of a public death for subsequent belief in the resurrection, it would surely have been better for him to have arranged an honorable death for himself, and so to have avoided the shame of the cross. But even this would have given ground for suspicion that his power over death was limited to the particular kind of death which he chose for himself; and that again would furnish excuse for disbelieving the resurrection. Death came to his body, therefore, not from himself but from enemy action, in order that the Savior might utterly abolish death in whatever form they offered it to him. A generous wrestler, virile and strong, does not himself choose his adversaries, lest it should be thought that of some of them he is afraid. Rather, he lets the spectators choose them, and that all the more if these are hostile, so that he may overthrow whomever they match against him and thus vindicate his superior strength. Even so was it with Christ. He, the Life of all, our Lord and Savior, did not arrange the manner of his own death lest he should seem to be afraid of some other kind. No—he accepted and bore upon the cross a death inflicted by others, and those others his special enemies, a death which to them was supremely terrible and by no means to be faced; and he did this in order that, by destroying even this death, he might himself be believed to be the Life, and the power of death be recognized as finally annulled. A marvelous and mighty paradox has thus occurred, for the death which they thought to inflict on him as dishonor and disgrace has become the glorious monument to death's defeat. Therefore it is also, that he neither endured the death of John, who was beheaded, nor was he sawn asunder, like Isaiah: even in death he preserved his body whole and undivided, so that there should be no excuse hereafter for those who would divide the church.

A marvelous and mighty paradox has thus occurred, for the death which they thought to inflict on him as dishonor and disgrace has become the glorious monument to death's defeat.

---

§25 – Why Jesus Had to Die by Crucifixion

So much for the objections of those outside the church. But if any honest Christian wants to know why he suffered death on the cross and not in some other way, we answer thus: in no other way was it expedient for us. Indeed, the Lord offered for our sakes the one death that was supremely good. He had come to bear the curse that lay on us; and how could he "become a curse" (Gal 3:13) otherwise than by accepting the accursed death? And that death is the cross, for it is written, "Cursed is everyone who is hanged on a tree" (Gal 3:13). Again, the death of the Lord is the ransom of all, and by it "the dividing wall of hostility" (Eph 2:14) is broken down and the call of the gentiles comes about. How could he have called us if he had not been crucified? For it is only on the cross that a man dies with arms outstretched. Here, again, we see the fitness of his death and of those outstretched arms: it was that he might draw his ancient people with the one and the gentiles with the other, and join both together in himself. Even so, he foretold the manner of his redeeming death, "And I, when I am lifted up from the

The cross is the glorious monument to death's defeat.

earth, will draw all people to myself" (John 12:32). Again, the air is the sphere of the devil, the enemy of our race who, having fallen from heaven, endeavors with the other evil spirits who shared in his disobedience both to keep souls from the truth and to hinder the progress of those who are trying to follow it. The apostle refers to this when he says, "following the prince of the power of the air, the spirit that is now at work in the sons of disobedience" (Eph 2:2). But the Lord came to overthrow the devil, to purify the air, and to make a way for us up to heaven, as the apostle says, "through the curtain, that is, through his flesh" (Heb 10:20). This had to be done through death, and by what other kind of death could it be done, except by a death in the air, that is, on the cross? Here, again, you see how right and natural it was that the Lord should suffer thus; for being thus "lifted up," he cleansed the air from all the evil influences of the enemy. "I saw Satan fall like lightning from heaven" (Luke 10:18), he says; and thus he reopened the road to heaven, saying again, "Lift up your heads, O gates! And be lifted up, O ancient doors" (Ps 24:7). For it was not the Word himself who needed an opening of the gates, he being Lord of all, nor was any of his works closed to their Maker. No, it was we who needed it, we whom he himself upbore in his own body—that body which he first offered to death on behalf of all, and then made through it a path to heaven.

Discussion Questions

 What is unique about crucifixion compared to other forms of death? What is the significance of Jesus dying particularly by means of crucifixion?

 Based on §20, what did Christ accomplish through his death on the cross?

 How does it make you feel knowing that Jesus bore your shame so that you can receive his honor?

 To "take up your cross" means to embrace the shame and hardships that come with a life of following Jesus. What shame or hardships are you experiencing as a result of your faith? How does Christ's victory on the cross give you perspective on those situations?

 How would your life be different if you began every day with a commitment to deny yourself, take up your cross, and follow Jesus?

Theology & Ethics

Chapter 5
The Resurrection of Christ

The destruction of death was accomplished through the cross of Christ. The resurrection, according to Athanasius, is a pledge and token of the victory of the cross. In other words, the resurrection reveals and inaugurates the salvation achieved through the crucifixion of Christ. And because death has been defeated, followers of Jesus do not need to live in fear, not even of death, for they have eternal life. The greatest evidence for the resurrection, argues Athanasius, is the works of the risen Christ today in the lives of believers and throughout the world. The resurrection of Jesus is the firstfruits of the incorruptible new creation.

***

§26 – The Resurrection as the Pledge of Christ's Victory on the Cross

Fitting indeed, then, and wholly consonant was the death on the cross for us; and we can see how reasonable it was, and why it is that the salvation of the world could be accomplished in no other way. Even on the cross he did not hide himself from sight; rather, he made all creation witness to the presence of its Maker. Then, having once let it be seen that it was truly dead, he did not allow that temple of his body to linger long, but immediately on the third day raised it up, impassable and incorruptible, the pledge and token of his victory.

It was, of course, within his power thus to have raised his body and displayed it as alive directly after death. But the all-wise Savior did not do this, lest some should deny that it had really or completely died. Besides this, had the interval between his death and resurrection been but two days, the glory of his incorruption might not have appeared. He waited one whole day to show that his body was really dead, and then on the third day showed it incorruptible to all. The interval was no longer, lest people should have forgotten about it and grown doubtful whether it were in truth the same body. No, while the affair was still ringing in their ears and their eyes were still straining and their minds in turmoil, and while those who had put him to death were still on the spot and themselves witnessing to the fact of it, the Son of God after three days showed his once dead body immortal and incorruptible; and it was evident to all that it was from no natural weakness that the body which the Word indwelt had died, but in order that in it, by the Savior's power, death might be done away.

§27 – No Fear of Death

A very strong proof of this destruction of death and its conquest by the cross is supplied by a present fact, namely this: all the disciples of Christ despise death; they take the offensive against it and, instead of fearing it, by the sign of the cross and by faith in Christ trample on it as on something dead. Before the divine sojourn of the Savior, even the holiest of people were afraid of death and mourned the dead as those who perish. But now that the Savior has raised his body, death is no longer terrible, but all those who believe in Christ tread it underfoot as nothing and prefer to die rather than to deny their faith in Christ, knowing full well that when they die, they do not perish but live indeed, and become incorruptible through the resurrection. But that devil who of old wickedly exulted in death, now that the pains of death are loosed, he alone it is who remains truly dead. There is proof of this too; for people who, before they believe in Christ, think death horrible and are afraid of it, once they are converted despise it so completely that they go eagerly to meet it, and themselves become witnesses of the Savior's resurrection from it. Even children hurry thus to die, and not men only, but women train themselves by bodily discipline to meet it. So weak has death become that even women, who used to be taken in by it, mock at it now as a dead thing robbed of all its strength. Death has become like a tyrant who has been completely conquered by the legitimate monarch; bound hand and foot the passersby sneer at him, hitting him and abusing him, no longer afraid of his cruelty and rage, because of the king who has conquered him. So has death been conquered and branded for what it is by the Savior on the cross. It is bound hand and foot; all who are in Christ trample it as they pass and as witnesses to him mock it, scoffing and saying, "O death, where is your victory? O death, where is your sting" (1 Cor 15:55)?

§28 – The Conquest of Death

Is this a slender proof of the impotence of death, do you think? Or is it a slight indication of the Savior's victory over it, when boys and young girls who are in Christ look beyond this present life and train themselves to die? Everyone is by nature afraid of death and of bodily dissolution; the marvel of marvels is that he who is enfolded in the faith of the cross despises this natural fear and for the sake of the cross is no longer cowardly in the face of it. The natural property of fire is to burn. Suppose, then, that there was a substance such as the Indian asbestos[1] is said to be, which had no fear of being burnt, but rather displayed the impotence of the fire by proving itself unburnable. If anyone doubted the truth of this, all he need do would be to wrap himself up in the substance in question and then touch the fire. Or, again, to revert to our former figure, if anyone wanted to see the tyrant bound and helpless, who used to be such a terror to others, he could do so simply by going into the country of the tyrant's conqueror. Even so, if anyone still doubts the conquest of death, after so many proofs and so many martyrdoms in Christ and such daily scorn of death by his truest servants, he certainly does well to marvel at so great a thing, but he must not be obstinate in unbelief and disregard of plain facts. No, he must be like the man who wants to prove the property of the asbestos,* and like him who enters the conqueror's dominions to see the tyrant bound. He must embrace the faith of Christ, this disbeliever in the conquest of death, and come to his teaching. Then he will see how death is impotent and completely conquered. Indeed, there have been many former unbelievers and mockers who, after they became

---

1   Asbestos – A mineral known for being fire-resistant.

believers, so scorned death as even themselves to become martyrs for Christ's sake.

§29 – Trampling Death

If, then, it is by the sign of the cross and by faith in Christ that death is trampled underfoot, it is clear that it is Christ himself and none other who is the supreme victor over death and has robbed it of its power. Death used to be strong and terrible, but now, since the sojourn of the Savior and the death and resurrection of his body, it is despised; and obviously it is by the very Christ who mounted on the cross that it has been destroyed and vanquished finally. When the sun rises after the night and the whole world is lit up by it, nobody doubts that it is the sun which has thus shed its light everywhere and driven away the dark. Equally clear is it, since this utter scorning and trampling down of death has ensued upon the Savior's manifestation in the body and his death on the cross, that it is he himself who brought death to nothing and daily raises monuments to his victory in his own disciples. How can you think otherwise, when you see people naturally weak hastening to death, unafraid at the prospect of corruption, fearless of the descent into Hades, even indeed with eager soul provoking it, not shrinking from tortures, but preferring thus to rush on to death for Christ's sake, rather than to remain in this present life? If you see with your own eyes men, women, and even children thus welcoming death for the sake of Christ's religion, how can you be so utterly silly and incredulous and maimed in your mind as not to realize that Christ, to whom these all bear witness, himself gives the victory to each, making death completely powerless for those who hold his faith and bear the sign of the cross? No one in his senses doubts that a snake is dead when he sees it trampled underfoot, especially when he knows how savage it used to be; nor, if he sees boys making fun of a lion, does he doubt that the brute is either dead or completely bereft of strength. These things can be seen with our own eyes, and it is the same with the conquest of death. Doubt no longer, then, when you see death mocked and scorned by those who believe in Christ, that by Christ death was destroyed, and the corruption that goes with it resolved and brought to end.

The cross of the Lord is the monument to his victory.

---

§30 – Christ's Resurrection Proven through the Transformed Lives of Believers

What we have said is, indeed, no small proof of the destruction of death and of the fact that the cross of the Lord is the monument to his victory. But the resurrection of the body to immortality, which results after this from the work of Christ, the common Savior and true Life of all, is more effectively proved by facts than by words to those whose mental vision is sound. For if, as we have shown, death was destroyed and everybody tramples on it because of Christ, how much more did he himself first trample and destroy it in his own body! Death having been slain by him, then, what other issue could there be than the resurrection of his body and its open demonstration as the monument of his victory? How could the destruction of death have been manifested at all, had not the Lord's body been raised? But if anyone finds even this insufficient, let him find proof of what has been said in present facts. Dead people cannot take effective action; their power of influence on others lasts only till the grave. Deeds and actions that energize others belong only to the living. Well, then, look at the facts in this case. The Savior is working mightily among humanity; every day he is invisibly persuading numbers of people all over the world, both within and beyond the Greek-speaking world, to accept his faith and be obedient to his teaching. Can anyone, in the face of this, still doubt that he has risen and lives, or rather that he is himself the Life? Does a dead man prick the consciences of people, so that they throw all the traditions of their fathers to the winds and bow down before the teaching of Christ? If he is no longer active in the world, as he must be if he is dead, how is it that he makes the living to cease from their activities, the adulterer from his adultery, the murderer from murdering, the unjust from greed, while the profane and godless man becomes religious? If he did not rise, but is still dead, how is it that he routs and persecutes and overthrows the false gods, whom unbelievers think to be alive, and the evil spirits whom they worship? For where Christ is named, idolatry is destroyed and the fraud of evil spirits is exposed; indeed, no such spirit can endure that name, but takes to flight on sound of it. This is the work of One who lives, not of one dead; and, more than that, it is the work of God. It would be absurd to say that the evil spirits whom he drives out and the idols which he destroys are alive, but that he who drives out and destroys, and whom they themselves acknowledge to be Son of God, is dead.

§31 – Christ's Resurrection Proven through His Works Today

In a word, then, those who disbelieve in the resurrection have no support in facts, if their gods and evil spirits do not drive away the supposedly dead Christ. Rather, it is he who convicts them of being dead. We are agreed that a dead person can do nothing: yet the Savior works mightily every day, drawing people to religion, persuading them to virtue, teaching them about immortality, quickening their thirst for heavenly things, revealing the knowledge of the Father, inspiring strength in face of death, manifesting himself to each, and displacing the irreligion of idols, while the gods and evil spirits of the unbelievers can do none of these things, but rather become dead at Christ's presence, all their ostentation barren and void. By the sign of the cross, on the contrary, all magic ceases, all sorcery is confounded, all idols are abandoned and deserted, and all senseless pleasure ceases, as the eye of faith looks up from earth to heaven. Whom, then, are we to call dead? Shall we call Christ dead, who effects all this? But the dead have not the faculty to effect anything. Or shall we call death dead, which effects nothing whatsoever, but lies as lifeless and ineffective as the evil spirits and the idols? The Son of God, "living and active" (Heb 4:12), is active every day and effects the salvation of all; but death is daily proved to be stripped of all its strength, and it is the idols and the evil spirits who are dead, not he. No room for doubt remains, therefore, concerning the resurrection of his body.

Indeed, it would seem that he who disbelieves this bodily rising of the Lord is ignorant of the power of the Word and Wisdom of God. If he took a body to himself at all, and made it his own in pursuance of his purpose, as we have shown that he did, what was the Lord to do with it, and what was ultimately to become of that body upon which the Word had descended? Mortal and offered to death on behalf of all as it was, it could not but die; indeed, it was for that very purpose that the Savior had prepared it for himself. But on the other hand it could not remain dead, because it had become the very temple of Life. It therefore died, as mortal, but lived again because of the Life within it; and its resurrection is made known through its works.

§32 – Christ's Resurrection Proven through His Power Manifested

It is, indeed, in accordance with the nature of the invisible God that he should be thus known through his works; and those who doubt the Lord's resurrection because they do not now behold him with their eyes might as well deny the very laws of nature. They have ground for disbelief when works are lacking; but when the works cry out and prove the fact so clearly, why do they deliberately deny the risen life so manifestly shown? Even if their mental faculties are defective, surely their eyes can give them irrefutable proof of the power and divinity of Christ. A blind man cannot see the sun, but he knows that it is above the earth from the warmth which it affords; similarly, let those who are still in the blindness of unbelief recognize the divinity of Christ and the resurrection which he has brought about through his manifested power in others. Obviously, he would not be expelling evil spirits and despoiling idols if he were dead, for the evil spirits would not obey one who was dead. If, on the other hand, the very naming of him drives them forth, he clearly is not dead; and the more so that the spirits, who perceive things unseen by people, would know if he were so and would refuse to obey him. But, as a matter of fact, what profane persons doubt, the evil spirits know—namely, that he is God—and for that reason they flee from him and fall at his feet, crying out even as they cried when he was in the body, "I know who you are—the Holy One of God" (Luke 4:34) and, "What

A blind man cannot see the sun, but he knows that it is above the earth from the warmth which it affords.

have you to do with me, Jesus, Son of the Most High God? I adjure you by God, do not torment me" (Mark 5:7).

Both from the confession of the evil spirits and from the daily witness of his works, it is manifest, then, and let none presume to doubt it, that the Savior has raised his own body, and that he is the very Son of God, having his being from God as from a Father, whose Word, Wisdom, and Power he is. He it is who in these latter days assumed a body for the salvation of us all and taught the world concerning the Father. He it is who has destroyed death and freely graced us all with incorruption through the promise of the resurrection, having raised his own body as its firstfruits and displayed it by the sign of the cross as the monument to his victory over death and its corruption.

Discussion Questions

 Athanasius says the greatest proof of the resurrection is Christ's work in our lives today. Where do you see evidence of the resurrected Jesus in your life and in the lives of others?

 When Jesus died on the cross, how did most people at the time view what was happening? How did the resurrection change the believers' perspective about the cross?

 Have you thought much about death? Are you afraid of dying? How does the resurrection of Jesus give us confidence even in the face of death?

 The apostle Paul says, "I have been crucified with Christ. It is no longer I who live, but Christ who lives in me" (Gal 2:20). How could this truth transform the way you live this week?

 Did you know that the church gathers on Sunday because that is the day Jesus rose from the grave? Why is gathering with the church every Sunday so important? How can it shape your heart and your character over time?

Chapter 6
Refutation of the Jews

Having set forth the incarnation of Christ, including the good news of his death and resurrection, Athanasius now anticipates the questions and criticisms that come from Jews and gentiles. First, he refutes the Jews by showing that the entire Old Testament is fulfilled in Christ's life, death, and resurrection. For Athanasius, Jesus is the Jewish messiah who fulfills every promise of God to save people from sin and renew creation.

***

§33 – The Old Testament Declares Christ

We have dealt thus far with the incarnation of our Savior, and have found clear proof of the resurrection of his body and his victory over death. Let us now go further and investigate the unbelief and the ridicule with which Jews and gentiles respectively regard these same facts. It seems that in both cases the points at issue are the same, namely the unfittingness or incongruity (as it seems to them) alike of the cross and of the Word's becoming man at all. But we have no hesitation in taking up the argument against these objectors, for the proofs on our side are extremely clear.

First, then, we will consider the Jews. Their unbelief has its refutation in the Scriptures which even themselves read; for from cover to cover the inspired book clearly teaches these things both in its entirety and in its actual words. Prophets foretold the marvel of the Virgin and of the birth from her, saying, "Behold, the virgin shall conceive and bear a son, and shall call his name Immanuel" (Isa 7:14), "which means, God with us" (Matt 1:23). And Moses, that truly great one in whose word the Jews trust so implicitly, he also recognized the importance and truth of the matter. He puts it thus: "A star shall come out of Jacob, and a scepter shall rise out of Israel; it shall crush the forehead of Moab" (Num 24:17). And again, "How lovely are your tents, O Jacob, your encampments, O Israel! Like palm groves that stretch afar, like gardens beside a river, like aloes that the Lord has planted, like cedar trees beside the waters. Water shall flow from his buckets, and his seed shall be in many waters" (Num 24:5–7). And again Isaiah says, "Before the boy knows how to cry 'My father' or 'My mother,' the wealth of Damascus and the spoil of Samaria will be carried away before the king of Assyria" (Isa 8:4). These words, then, foretell that a man shall appear. And Scripture proclaims further that he that is to come is Lord of all. These are the words, "Behold, the Lord is riding on a swift cloud and comes to Egypt; and the idols of Egypt will tremble at his presence" (Isa 19:1). And it is from Egypt also that the Father calls him back, saying, "Out of Egypt I called my son" (Hos 11:1).

§34 – The Old Testament Foretells Christ's Death for Us

Moreover, the Scriptures are not silent even about his death. On the contrary, they refer to it with the utmost clearness. They have not feared to speak also of the cause of it. He endures it, they say, not for his own sake, but for the sake of bringing immortality and salvation to all, and they record also the plotting of the Jews against him and all the indignities which he suffered at their hands. Certainly nobody who reads the Scriptures can plead ignorance of the facts as an excuse for error! There is this passage, for instance: "He was despised and rejected by men, a man of sorrows and acquainted with grief; and as one from whom men hide their faces he was despised, and we esteemed him not. Surely, he has borne our griefs and carried our sorrows; yet we esteemed him stricken, smitten by God, and afflicted. But he was pierced for our transgressions; he was crushed for our iniquities; upon him was the chastisement that brought us peace, and with his wounds we are healed" (Isa 53:3–5). Marvel at the love of the Word for humanity, for it is on our account that he is dishonored, so that we may be brought to honor. "All we," it goes on, "like sheep have gone astray; we have turned—every one—to his own way; and the Lord has laid on him the iniquity of us all. He was oppressed, and he was afflicted, yet he opened not his mouth; like a lamb that is led to the slaughter, and like a sheep that before its shearers is silent, so he opened not his mouth. By oppression and judgment he was taken away" (Isa 53:6–8). And then Scripture anticipates the surmises of any who might think from his suffering thus that he was just an ordinary man, and shows what power worked in his behalf. "As for his generation, who considered that he was cut off out of the land of the living, stricken for the transgression of my people?" It says, "By oppression and judgment he was taken away; . . . and they made his grave with the wicked and with a rich man in his death, although he had done no violence, and there was no deceit in his mouth. Yet it was the will of the Lord to crush him" (Isa 53:8–10).

§35 – The Old Testament Prophecies the Cross and Virgin Birth

You have heard the prophecy of his death, and now, perhaps, you want to know what indications there are about the cross. Even this is not passed over in silence: on the contrary, the sacred writers proclaim it with the utmost plainness. Moses foretells it first, and that right loudly, when he says, "Your life shall hang in doubt before you . . . you shall be in dread and have no assurance of your life" (Deut 28:66). After him the prophets also give their witness, saying, "But I was like a gentle lamb led to the slaughter. I did not know it was against me they devised schemes, saying, 'Let us destroy the tree with its fruit, let us cut him off from the land of the living'" (Jer 11:19). And, again, "They have pierced my hands and feet—I can count all my bones—they stare and gloat over me; they divide my garments among them, and for my clothing they cast lots" (Ps 22:16–18). Now a death lifted up and that takes place on wood can be none other than the death of the cross; moreover, it is only in that death that the hands and feet are pierced. Besides this, since the Savior dwelt among humanity, all nations everywhere have begun to know God; and this too Holy Scripture expressly mentions. "In that day the root of Jesse, who shall stand as a signal for the peoples—of him shall the nations inquire, and his resting place shall be glorious" (Isa 11:10).

These are just a few things in proof of what has taken place; but indeed all Scripture teems with disproof of Jewish unbelief. For example, which of the righteous men and holy prophets and patriarchs of whom the divine Scriptures tell ever had his bodily birth from a virgin only? Was not Abel born of Adam, Enoch of Jared, Noah of Lamech, Abraham of Terah, Isaac of Abraham, and Jacob of Isaac? Was not Judah begotten by Jacob, and Moses and Aaron by Ameram? Was not Samuel the son of Elkanah, David of Jesse, Solomon of David, Hezekiah of Ahaz, Josiah of Amon, Isaiah of Amos, Jeremiah of Hilkiah, and Ezekiel of Buzi? Had not each of these a father as author of his being? So who is he that is born of a virgin only, that sign of which the prophet makes so much? Again, which of all those people had his birth announced to the world by a star in the heavens? When Moses was born his parents hid him. David was unknown even in his own neighborhood, so that mighty Samuel himself was ignorant of his existence and asked whether Jesse had yet another son. Abraham again became known to his neighbors as a great man only after his birth. But with Christ it was otherwise. The witness to his birth was not a man, but a star shining in the heavens from where he was coming down.

§36 – Jesus Is Greater than Abraham, Moses, and David

Then, again, what king that ever was reigned and took trophies from his enemies before he had strength to call father or mother? Was not David thirty years old when he came to the throne and Solomon a grown young man? Did not Joash enter on his reign at the age of seven, and Josiah, sometime after him, at about the same age, both

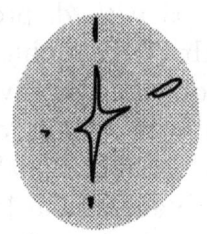

The witness to Christ's birth was not a man, but a star shining in the heavens.

of them fully able by that time to call father or mother? Who is there, then, that was reigning and despoiling his enemies almost before he was born? Let the Jews, who have investigated the matter, tell us if there was ever such a king in Israel or Judah—a king upon whom all the nations set their hopes and had peace, instead of being at war with him on every side! As long as Jerusalem stood there was constant war between them, and they all fought against Israel. The Assyrians oppressed Israel, the Egyptians persecuted them, the Babylonians fell upon them, and, strange to relate, even the Syrians their neighbors were at war with them. And did not David fight with Moab and strike the Syrians, and Hezekiah shake at the boasting of Sennacherib? Did not Amalek make war on Moses and the Amorites oppose him, and did not the inhabitants of Jericho array themselves against Joshua the son of Nun? Did not the nations always regard Israel with implacable hostility? Then it is worth inquiring who it is, on whom the nations are to set their hopes. Obviously there must be someone, for the prophet could not have told a lie. But did any of the holy prophets or of the early patriarchs die on the cross for the salvation of all? Was any of them wounded and killed for the healing of all? Did the idols of Egypt fall down before any righteous man or king that came there? Abraham came there certainly, but idolatry prevailed just the same; and Moses was born there, but the mistaken worship was unchanged.

§37 – Jesus Is the Fulfillment of the Old Testament

Again, does Scripture tell of anyone who was pierced in hands and feet or hung upon a tree at all, and by means of a cross perfected his sacrifice for the salvation of all? It was not Abraham, for he died in his bed, as did also

Isaac and Jacob. Moses and Aaron died on the mountain, and David ended his days in his house, without anybody having plotted against him. Certainly he had been sought by Saul, but he was preserved unharmed. Again Isaiah was sawn in half, but he was not hung on a tree. Jeremiah was shamefully used, but he did not die under condemnation. Ezekiel suffered, but he did so not on behalf of the people, but only to signify to them what was going to happen. Moreover, all these even when they suffered were but men, like other men; but he whom the Scriptures declare to suffer on behalf of all is called not merely man but Life of all, although in point of fact he did share our human nature. "Your life shall hang in doubt before you" (Deut 28:66), they say, and "as for his generation, who considered that he was cut off out of the land of the living, stricken for the transgression of my people?" (Isa 53:8). With all the saints we can trace their descent from the beginning, and see exactly how each came to be; but the divine Word maintains that we cannot declare the lineage of him who is the Life. Who is it, then, of whom Holy Scripture thus speaks? Who is there so great that even the prophets foretell of him such mighty things? There is indeed no one in the Scriptures at all, except the common Savior of all, the Word of God, our Lord Jesus Christ. He it is that proceeded from a virgin and appeared as man on earth, he it is whose earthly lineage cannot be declared, because he alone derives his body from no human father but from a virgin alone. We can trace the paternal descent of David and Moses and of all the patriarchs. But with the Savior we cannot do so, for it was he himself who caused the star to announce his bodily birth, and it was fitting that the Word, when he came down from heaven, should have his sign in heaven too, and fitting that the King of creation on his coming forth should be visibly recognized by all the world. He was actually born in Judea, yet men from Persia came to worship him. He it is who won victory from his demon foes and trophies from the idolaters even before his bodily appearing—namely, all the pagans who from every region have renounced the tradition of their fathers and the false worship of idols and are now placing their hope in Christ and transferring their allegiance to him. The thing is happening before our very eyes, here in Egypt; and thereby another prophecy is fulfilled, for at no other time have the Egyptians ceased from their false worship except when the Lord of all, riding as on a cloud, came down here in the body and brought the error of idols to nothing and won over everybody to himself and through himself to the Father. He it is who was crucified with the sun and moon as witnesses; and by his death salvation has come to all people, and all creation has been redeemed. He is the Life of all, and he it is who like a sheep gave up his own body to death, his life for ours and our salvation.

§38 – Jesus Is the Fulfillment of the Prophets

Yet the Jews disbelieve this. This argument does not satisfy them. Well, then, let them be persuaded by other things in their own oracles. Of whom, for instance, do the prophets say "I was ready to be sought by those who did not ask for me; I was ready to be found by those who did not seek me. I said, 'Here I am, here I am,' to a nation that was not called by my name. I spread out my hands all the day to a rebellious people" (Isa 65:1–2). Who is this person that was made manifest, one might ask the Jews? If the prophet is speaking of himself, then they must tell us how he was first hidden, in order to be manifested afterward. And again, what kind of man is this prophet, who was not only revealed after being hidden, but also stretched out his hands upon the cross? Those things happened to none of those righteous men: they happened only to the Word of God who, being by nature without body, on our account appeared in a body and suffered for us all. And if even this is not enough for them, there is other overwhelming evidence by which they may be silenced. The Scripture says, "Strengthen the weak hands, and make firm the feeble knees. Say to those who have an anxious heart, 'Be strong; fear not! Behold, your God will come with vengeance, with the recompense of God. He will come and save you.' Then the eyes of the blind shall be opened, and the ears of the deaf unstopped; then shall the lame man leap like a deer, and the tongue of the mute sing for joy" (Isa 35:3–6). What can they say to this, or how can they look it in the face at all? For the prophecy does not only declare that God will dwell here, it also makes known the signs and the time of his coming. When God comes, it says, the blind will see, the lame will walk, the deaf will hear and the stammerers will speak distinctly. Can the Jews tell us when such signs occurred in Israel, or when anything of the kind took place at all in Judah? The leper Naaman was cleansed, it is true (2 Kgs 5:1–14), but no deaf man heard nor did any lame man walk. Elijah raised a dead person (1 Kgs 17:17–24), and so did Elisha (2 Kgs 4:18–37); but no one blind from birth received his sight. To raise a dead person is a great thing indeed, but it is not such as the Savior did. And surely, since the Scriptures have not kept silence about the leper and the dead son of the widow, if a lame man had walked and a blind man had received his sight, they would have mentioned these as well. Their silence on these points proves that the events never took place. When therefore did these things happen, unless when the Word of God himself came in the body? Was it not when he came that the lame walked and stammerers spoke clearly and people blind from birth were given sight? And the Jews who saw it themselves testified to the fact that such things had never before occurred. "Never since the world began has it been heard that anyone opened the eyes of a man born blind. If this man were not from God, he could do nothing" (John 9:32–33).

§39 – Jesus Is the "Anointed One" from the Book of Daniel

But surely they cannot fight against plain facts. So it may be that, without denying what is written, they will maintain that they are still waiting for these things to happen, and that the Word of God is yet to come, for that is a theme on which they are always harping most brazenly, in spite of all the evidence against them. But they shall be refuted on this supreme point more clearly than on any, and that not by ourselves but by the most wise Daniel, for he signifies the actual date of the Savior's coming as well as his divine sojourn in our midst. "Seventy weeks are decreed about your people and your holy city, to finish the transgression, to put an end to sin, and to atone for iniquity, to bring in everlasting righteousness, to seal both vision and prophet, and to anoint a most holy place. Know therefore and understand that from the going out of the word to restore and build Jerusalem to the coming of an anointed one, a prince, there shall be seven weeks" (Dan 9:24–25). In regard to the other prophecies, they may possibly be able to find excuses for deferring their reference to a future time, but what can they say to this one? How can they face it at all? Not only does it expressly mention the Anointed One, that is the Christ, it even declares that he who is to be anointed is not man only, but the Holy One of holies! And it says that Jerusalem is to stand till his coming, and that after it prophet and vision shall cease in Israel! David was anointed of old, and Solomon, and Hezekiah; but then Jerusalem and the place stood, and prophets were prophesying, Gad and Asaph and Nathan, and later Isaiah and Hosea and Amos and others. Moreover, those men who were anointed were called holy certainly, but none of them was called the Holy of holies. Nor is it any use for the Jews to take refuge in the captivity, and say that Jerusalem did not exist then, for what about the prophets? It is a fact that at the outset of the exile, Daniel and Jeremiah were there, and Ezekiel, Haggai, and Zechariah also prophesied.

§40 – The Jewish Messiah Has Already Come

So the Jews are indulging in fiction, and transferring present time to future. When did prophet and vision cease from Israel? Was it not when Christ, the Holy of holies, came? It is, in fact, a sign and notable proof of the coming of the Word that Jerusalem no longer stands, neither is prophet raised up nor vision revealed among them. And it is natural that it should be so, for when he that was signified had come, what need was there any longer of any to signify him? And when the Truth had come, what further need was there of the shadow? On his account only they prophesied continually, until such time as Justice itself has come, who was made the Ransom for the sins of all. For the same reason Jerusalem stood until the same time, in order that there men might premeditate the types before the Truth was known. So, of course, once the Holy One of holies had come, both vision and prophecy were sealed. And the kingdom of Jerusalem ceased at the same time, because kings were to be anointed among them only

Chapter 6: Refutation of the Jews

until the Holy of holies had been anointed. Moses also prophesies that the kingdom of the Jews shall stand until his time, saying, "The scepter shall not depart from Judah, nor the ruler's staff from between his feet, until tribute comes to him; and to him shall be the obedience of the peoples" (Gen 49:10). And that is why the Savior himself was always proclaiming, "For all the Prophets and the Law prophesied until John" (Matt 11:13). So if there is still king, or prophet, or vision among the Jews, they do well to deny that Christ is come; but if there is neither king nor vision, and since that time all prophecy has been sealed and city and temple taken, how can they be so irreligious, how can they so flaunt the facts, as to deny Christ who has brought it all about? Again, they see the pagans forsaking idols and setting their hopes through Christ on the God of Israel; why do they yet deny Christ who after the flesh was born of the root of Jesse and reigns from this point on? Of course, if the pagans were worshiping some other god, and not confessing the God of Abraham and Isaac and Jacob and Moses, then they would do well to argue that God had not come. But if the heathen are honoring the same God who gave the law to Moses and the promises to Abraham—the God whose word too the Jews dishonored, why do they not recognize—or rather why do they deliberately refuse to see—that the Lord of whom the Scriptures prophesied has shone forth to the world and appeared to it in a bodily form? Scripture declares it repeatedly. "The Lord is God, and he has made his light to shine upon us" (Ps 118:27), and again, "He sent out his word and healed them" (Ps 107:20). And again, "In all their affliction he was afflicted, and the angel of his presence saved them" (Isa 63:9). The Jews are afflicted like some demented person who sees the earth lit up by the sun, but denies the sun that lights it up!

What more is there for their Expected One to do when he comes? To call the pagans? But they are called already. To put an end to prophet and king and vision? But this too has already happened. To expose the God-denyingness of idols? It is already exposed and condemned. Or to destroy death? It is already destroyed. What then has not come to pass that the Christ must do? What is there left out or unfulfilled that the Jews should disbelieve so light-heartedly? The plain fact is, as I say, that there is no longer any king or prophet nor Jerusalem nor sacrifice nor vision among them; yet the whole earth is filled with the knowledge of God, and the gentiles, forsaking atheism, are now taking refuge with the God of Abraham through the Word, our Lord Jesus Christ.

> What then has not come to pass that the Christ must do?

Surely, then, it must be plain even to the most shameless that the Christ has come, and that he has enlightened all people everywhere, and given them the true and divine teaching about his Father.

Thus the Jews may be refuted by these and other arguments from the divine teaching.

Discussion Questions

 Why is it important for Christians to understand and respond to common criticisms of the faith?

 How have you typically thought of the way Jesus relates to the Old Testament? How is the Old Testament relevant for Christians today?

 Athanasius argues that Jesus is the fulfillment of God's promises in the Old Testament. What Old Testament promise do you most long for that is fulfilled in Jesus?

 Read 2 Corinthians 1:20. List out as many Old Testament promises (that you can think of) that Jesus fulfills.

 Do you incorporate the Old Testament into your rhythms of reading Scripture? If so, how has that helped you to further understand Jesus? If not, why do you think you have neglected the Old Testament? Are you willing to incorporate the Old Testament into your life?

Theology & Ethics

Chapter 7
Refutation of the Gentiles

After refuting the Jews, Athanasius anticipates the disagreements that will come from the gentiles. With Alexandria being a diverse and influential city, Athanasius needed to understand the beliefs of the pagans to persuade them about the good news of Jesus. He refutes the gentiles by demonstrating the reasonableness of the gospel and arguing that Jesus is greater than all power, magic, idols, and gods.

***

§41 – The Reasonableness of the Incarnation

We come now to the unbelief of the gentiles; and this is indeed a matter for complete astonishment, for they laugh at that which is no fit subject for mockery, yet fail to see the shame and ridiculousness of their own idols. But the arguments on our side do not lack weight, so we will confute them too on reasonable grounds, chiefly from what we ourselves also see.

First of all, what is there in our belief that is unfitting or ridiculous? Is it only that we say that the Word has been manifested in a body? Well, if they themselves really love the truth, they will agree with us that this involved no unfittingness at all. If they deny that there is a Word of God at all, that will be extraordinary, for then they will be ridiculing what they do not know. But suppose they confess that there is a Word of God, that he is the Governor of all things, that in him the Father made the creation, that by his providence the whole world receives light and life and being, and that he is King over all, so that he is known by means of the works of his providence, and through him the Father. Suppose they confess all this: what then? Are they not unknowingly turning the ridicule against themselves? The Greek philosophers say that the universe is a great body, and they say truly, for we perceive the universe and its parts with our senses. But if the Word of God is in the universe, which is a body, and has entered into it in its every part, what is there surprising or unfitting in our saying that he has entered also into human nature? If it were unfitting for him to have embodied himself at all, then it would be unfitting for him to have entered into the universe, and to be giving light and movement by his providence to all things in it, because the universe, as we have seen, is itself a body. But if it is right and fitting for him to enter into the universe and to reveal himself through it, then, because humanity is part of the universe along with the rest, it is no less fitting for him to appear in a human body, and to enlighten and to work through that. And surely if it were wrong for a part of the universe to have been used to reveal his divinity to people, it would be much more wrong that he should be so revealed by the whole!

§42 – Can Christ Pervade All Things and Be in a Body?

Take a parallel case. A man's personality actuates and quickens his whole body. If anyone said it was unsuitable for the man's power to be in the toe, he would be thought silly, because, while granting that a man penetrates and actuates the whole of his body, he denied his presence in the part. Similarly, no one who admits the presence of the Word of God in the universe as a whole should think it unsuitable for a single human body to be by him actuated and enlightened.

But is it, perhaps, because humanity is a thing created and brought into being out of nonexistence that they regard as unfitting the manifestation of the Savior in our nature? If so, it is high time that they spurned him from creation too; for it, too, has been brought out of nonbeing into being by the Word. But if, on the other hand, although creation is a thing that has been made, it is not unsuitable for the Word to be present in it, then neither is it unsuitable for him to be in man. Man is a part of the creation, as I said before; and the reasoning which applies to one applies to the other. All things derive from the Word their light and movement and life, as the gentile authors themselves say, "For 'In him we live and move and have our being'" (Acts 17:28). Very well then. That being so, it is by no means unbecoming that the Word should dwell in man. So if, as we say, the Word has used that in which he is as the means of his self-manifestation, what is there ridiculous in that? He could not have used it had he not been present in it; but we have already admitted that he is present both in the whole and in the parts. What, then, is there incredible in his manifesting himself through that in which he is? By his own power he enters completely into each and all, and orders them throughout ungrudgingly; and, had he so willed, he could have revealed himself and his Father by means of sun, moon, sky, earth, fire, or water. Had he done so, no one could rightly have accused him of acting unbecomingly, for he sustains in one whole all things at once, being present and invisibly revealed not only in the whole, but also in each particular part. This being so, and since, moreover, he has willed to reveal himself through people, who are part of the whole, there can be nothing ridiculous in his using a human body to manifest the truth and knowledge of the Father. Does not the mind of man pervade his entire being, and yet find expression through one part only, namely the tongue? Does anybody say on that account that Mind has degraded itself? Of course not. Very well, then: no more is it degrading for the Word, who pervades all things, to have appeared in a human body. For, as I said before, if it were unfitting for him thus to indwell the part, it would be equally so for him to exist within the whole.

§43 – Why Did God Not Enter Creation as Something Else?

Some may then ask, why did he not manifest himself by means of other and nobler parts of creation, and use some nobler instrument, such as sun, moon, stars, fire, or air, instead of mere man? The answer is this. The Lord did not come to make a display. He came to heal and to teach suffering people. For one who wanted to make a display, the thing would have been just to appear and dazzle the beholders. But for him who came to heal and to teach the way was not merely to dwell here, but to put himself at the disposal of those who needed him, and to be manifested accordingly, as they could bear it, not nullifying the value of the divine appearing by exceeding their capacity to receive it.

Moreover, nothing in creation had erred from the path of God's purpose for it, except only humanity. Sun, moon, heaven, stars, water, air—none of these had swerved from their order but, knowing the Word as their Maker and their King, remained as they were made. People alone, having rejected what is good, have invented nothings instead of the truth, and have ascribed the honor due to God and the knowledge concerning him to demons and people in the form of stones. Obviously the divine goodness could not overlook so grave a matter as this. But humanity could not recognize him as ordering and ruling creation as a whole. So what does he do? He takes to himself for instrument a part of the whole, namely a human body, and enters into that. Thus he ensured that humanity should recognize him in the part who could not do so in the whole, and that those who could not lift their eyes to his unseen power might recognize and behold him in the likeness of themselves. For, being human, they would naturally learn to know his Father more quickly and directly by means of a body that corresponded to their own and by the divine works done through it; for by comparing his works with their own they would judge his to be not human but divine. And if, as they say, it were unsuitable for the Word to reveal himself through bodily acts, it would be equally so for him to do so through the works of the universe. His being in creation does not mean that he shares its nature; on the contrary, all created things partake of his power. Similarly, though he used the body as his instrument, he shared nothing of the body's attributes, but rather sanctified it by his indwelling. Does not even Plato, of whom the Greeks think so much, say that the Author of the universe, seeing it storm-tossed and in danger of sinking into a state of dissolution, takes his seat at the helm of the life-force of the universe, comes to the rescue, and puts everything right? What, then, is there incredible in our saying that, humanity having gone astray, the Word descended upon it and was manifest as man, so that by his intrinsic goodness and his guidance he might save it from the storm?

§44 – Could God Not Save by His Will Alone?

It may be, however, that, though shamed into agreeing that this objection is void, the Greeks will want to raise another. They will say that, if God wanted to instruct and save humanity, he might have done so not by his Word's assumption of a body but, even as he at first created them, by the mere signification of his will. The reasonable reply is that the circumstances in the two cases are quite different. In the beginning, nothing as yet existed at all; all that was needed, therefore, in order to bring all things into being, was that his will to do so should be signified. But once humanity was in existence, and things that were, not things that were not, demanded to be healed, it followed as a matter of course that the Healer and Savior should align himself with those things that existed already, in order to heal the existing evil. For that reason, therefore, he was made man, and used the body as his human instrument. If this were not the fitting way, and he willed to use an instrument at all, how otherwise was the Word to come? And from where could he take his instrument, except from among those already in existence and needing his divinity through One like themselves? It was not things non-existent that needed salvation, for which a bare creative word might have sufficed, but humanity—people already in existence and already in process of corruption and ruin.

It was natural and right, therefore, for the Word to use a human instrument and by that means unfold himself to all.

Therefore he put on a body, so that in the body he might find death and blot it out.

You must know, moreover, that the corruption which had set in was not external to the body but established within it. The need, therefore, was that life should cleave to it in corruption's place, so that, just as death was brought into being in the body, life also might be engendered in it. If death had been exterior to the body, life might fittingly have been the same. But if death was within the body, woven into its very substance and dominating it as though completely one with it, the need was for Life to be woven into it instead, so that the body by thus enduing itself with life might cast corruption off. Suppose the Word had come outside the body instead of in it: he would, of course, have defeated death, because death is powerless against the Life. But the corruption inherent in the body would have remained in it nonetheless. Naturally, therefore, the Savior assumed a body for himself, in order that the body, being interwoven as it were with life, should no longer remain a mortal thing, under the power of death, but having put on immortality and risen from death, should then remain immortal. For once having put on corruption, it could not rise, unless it put on life instead; and besides this, death of its very nature could not appear otherwise than in a body. Therefore he put on a body, so that in the body he might find death and blot it out. And, indeed, how could the Lord have been proved to be the Life at all, unless he had given life to what was mortal? Take an illustration.

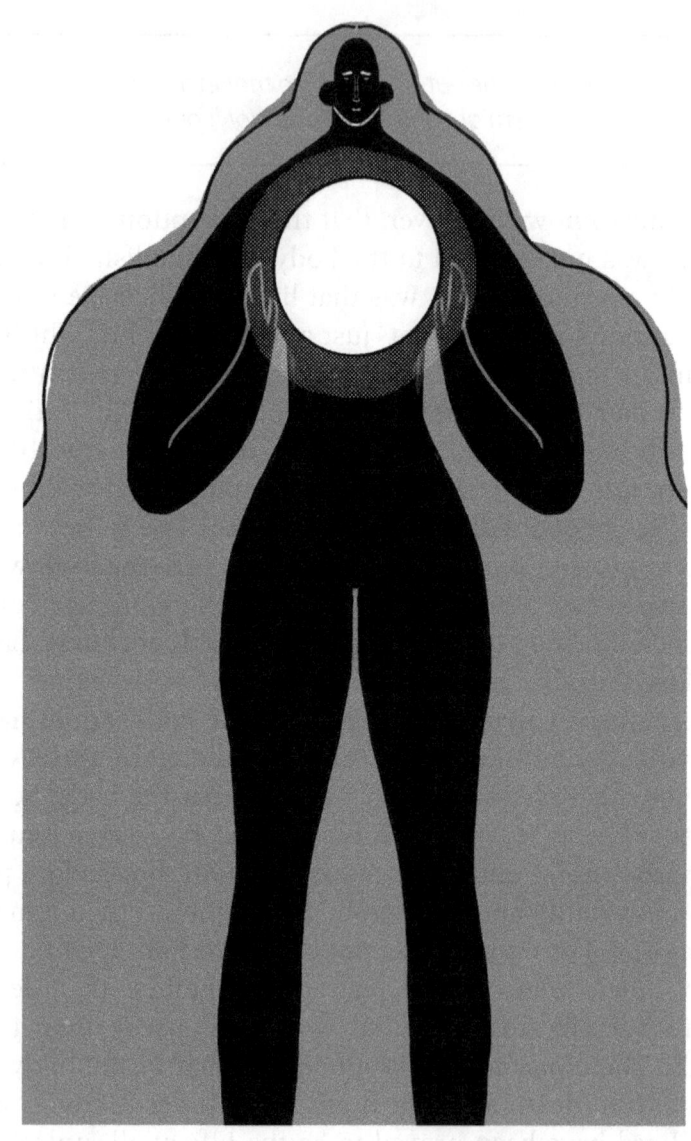

*But if death was within the body,
the need was for Life to be woven into it instead.*

Straw is a substance naturally destructible by fire; and it still remains straw, fearing the menace of fire which has the natural property of consuming it, even if fire is kept away from it, so that it is not actually burnt. But suppose that, instead of merely keeping the fire from it, somebody soaks the straw with a quantity of asbestos,* the substance which is said to be the antidote to fire. Then the straw no longer fears the fire because it has put on that which fire cannot touch, and therefore it is safe. It is just the same with regard to the body and death. Had death been kept from it by a mere command, it would still have remained mortal and corruptible according to its nature. To prevent this, it put on the incorporeal Word of God and therefore fears neither death nor corruption anymore, for it is clad with Life as with a garment and in it corruption is clean done away.

§45 – Christ in All of Creation

The Word of God thus acted consistently in assuming a body and using a human instrument to vitalize the body. He was consistent in working through humanity to reveal himself everywhere, as well as through the other parts of his creation, so that nothing was left void of his divinity and knowledge. For I take up now the point I made before, namely, that the Savior did this in order that he might fill all things everywhere with the knowledge of himself, just as they are already filled with his presence, even as the divine Scripture says, "The earth shall be full of the knowledge of the Lord" (Isa 11:9). If a man looks up to heaven he sees there his ordering; but if he cannot look so high as heaven, but only so far as people, through his works he sees his power, incomparable with human might, and learns from them that he alone among humanity is God the Word. Or, if a man has gone astray among demons and is in fear of them, he may see this man drive them out and judge from there that he is indeed their Master. Again, if a man has been immersed in the element of water and thinks that it is God—as indeed the Egyptians do worship water—he may see its very nature changed by him and learn that the Lord is Creator of all. And if a man has gone down even to Hades, and stands awestruck before the heroes who have descended there, regarding them as gods, still he may see the fact of Christ's resurrection and his victory over death, and reason from it that, of all these, he alone is very Lord and God.

For the Lord touched all parts of creation, and freed and undeceived them all from every deceit. As Paul says, "He disarmed the rulers and authorities and put them to open shame, by triumphing over them in him" (Col 2:15), so that no one could possibly be any longer deceived, but everywhere might find the very Word of God. For thus humanity, enclosed on every side by the works of creation and everywhere—in heaven, in Hades, in people, and on the earth—beholding the unfolded divinity of the Word, is no longer deceived concerning God, but worships Christ alone, and through him rightly knows the Father.

On these grounds, then, of reason and of principle, we will fairly silence the gentiles in their turn. But if they think these arguments insufficient to confute them, we will go on in the next chapter to prove our point from facts.

§46 – Jesus Is Greater than Idols

When did people begin to abandon the worship of idols, unless it was since the very Word of God came among humanity? When have oracles ceased and become void of meaning, among the Greeks and everywhere, except since the Savior has revealed himself on earth? When did those whom the poets call gods and heroes begin to be condemned as mere mortals, except when the Lord took the spoils of death and preserved incorruptible the body he had taken, raising it from among the dead? Or when did the deceitfulness and madness of demons fall under contempt, except when the Word, the Power of God, the Master of all these as well, condescended on account of the weakness of mankind and appeared on earth? When did the practice and theory of magic begin to be spurned under foot, if not at the manifestation of the divine Word to humanity? In a word, when did the wisdom of the Greeks become foolish, except when the true Wisdom of God revealed himself on earth? In old times the whole world and every place in it was led astray by the worship of idols, and people thought the idols were the only gods that were. But now all over the world people are forsaking the fear of idols and taking refuge with Christ; and by worshiping him as God they come through him to know the Father also, whom formerly they did not know. The amazing thing, moreover, is this: the objects of worship formerly were varied and countless; each place had its own idol and the so-called god of one place could not pass over to another in order to persuade the people there to worship him, but was barely reverenced even by his own. Indeed no! Nobody worshiped his neighbor's god, but everyone had his own idol and thought that it was lord of all. But now Christ alone is worshiped, as one and the same among all peoples everywhere; and what the feebleness of idols could not do, namely, convince even those dwelling close at hand, he has affected. He has persuaded not only those close at hand, but literally the entire world to worship one and the same Lord and through him the Father.

§47 – Jesus Is Greater than Demons

Again, in former times every place was full of the fraud of the oracles, and the utterances of those at Delphi and Dordona, in Boeotia, Lycia, Libya, and Egypt, and those of the Kabiri and the Pythoness were considered marvelous by the minds of people. But now, since Christ has been proclaimed everywhere, their madness too has ceased, and there is no one left among them to give oracles at all. Then, too, demons used to deceive people's minds by taking up their abode in springs, rivers, trees, or stones and imposing upon simple people by their frauds. But now, since the divine appearing of the Word, all this fantasy has ceased, for by the sign of the cross, if a man will but use it, he drives out their deceits. Again, people used to regard as gods those who are mentioned in the poets—Zeus, Kronos, Apollo, and the heroes—and in worshiping them they went astray. But now that the Savior has appeared among humanity, those others have been exposed as mortals, and Christ alone is recognized as true God, Word of God, God himself. And what is one to say about the magic that they think so marvelous? Before the sojourn of the Word, it was strong and active among Egyptians, Chaldeans, and Indians and filled all who saw it with terror and astonishment. But by the coming of the Truth and the manifestation of the Word it too has been confuted and entirely destroyed. As to Greek wisdom, however, and the philosophers' noisy talk, I really think no one requires argument from us; for the amazing fact is obvious to all that, for all that they had written so much, the Greeks failed to convince even a few from their own neighborhood in regard to immortality and the virtuous ordering of life. Christ alone, using common speech and through the agency of people not clever with their tongues, has convinced whole assemblies of people all the world over to despise death, and to take heed to the things that do not die, to look past the things of time and gaze on things eternal, to think nothing of earthly glory and to aspire only to immortality.

§48 – Jesus Is Greater than Magicians

These things which we have said are no mere words: they are attested by actual experience. Anyone who likes may see the proof of glory in the virgins of Christ, and in the young men who practice sexual purity as part of their religion, and in the assurance of immortality in so great and glad a company of martyrs. Anyone, too, may put what we have said to the proof of experience in another way. In the very presence of the fraud of demons and the imposture of the oracles and the wonders of magic, let him use the sign of the cross which they all mock at, and but speak the name of Christ, and he shall see how through him demons are routed, oracles cease, and all magic and witchcraft is confounded.

Who, then, is this Christ and how great is he, who by his name and presence overshadows and confounds all things on every side, who alone is strong against all and has filled the whole world with his teaching? Let the Greeks tell us, who mock at him without shame. If he is a man, how is it that one man has proved stronger than all those whom they themselves regard as gods and by his own power has shown them to be nothing? If they call him a magician, how is it that by a magician all magic is destroyed, instead of being rendered strong? Had he conquered certain magicians or proved himself superior to one of them only, they might reasonably think that he excelled the rest only by his greater skill. But the fact is that his cross has vanquished all magic entirely and has conquered the very name of it. Obviously, therefore, the Savior is no magician, for the very demons whom the magicians invoke flee from him as from their Master. Who is he, then? Let the Greeks tell us, whose only serious pursuit is mockery! Perhaps they will say that he, too, is a demon, and that is why he prevailed. But even so the laugh is still on our side, for we can confute them by the same proofs as before. How could he be a demon, who drives demons out? If it were only certain ones that he drove out, then they might reasonably think that he prevailed against them through the power of their chief, as the Jews, wishing to insult him, actually said. But since the fact is, here again, that at the mere naming of his name all madness of the demons is rooted out and put to flight, obviously the Greeks are wrong here, too, and our Lord and Savior Christ is not, as they maintain, some demonic power.

If, then, the Savior is neither a mere human nor a magician, nor one of the demons, but has by his divinity confounded and overshadowed the opinions of the poets, the delusion of the demons, and the wisdom of the Greeks, it must be manifest and will be owned by all that he is in truth Son of God, existent Word, Wisdom, and Power of the Father. This is the reason why his works are no mere human works, but, both intrinsically and by comparison with those of people, are recognized as being superhuman and truly the works of God.

§49 – Jesus Is Greater than Greek Gods

What man that ever was, for instance, formed a body for himself from a virgin only? Or what man ever healed so many diseases as the common Lord of all? Who restored that which was lacking in man's nature or made one blind from birth to see? Aesculapius[1] was deified by the Greeks because he practiced the art of healing and discovered herbs as remedies for bodily diseases, not, of course, forming them himself out of the earth, but finding them out by the study of nature. But what is that in comparison with what the Savior did when, instead of just healing a wound, he both fashioned essential being and restored to health the thing that he had formed? Hercules, too, is worshiped as a god by the Greeks because he fought against other men and destroyed wild animals by craft. But what is that to what the Word did in driving away from people diseases, demons, and even death itself? Dionysus is worshiped among them, because he taught people drunkenness; yet they ridicule the true Savior and Lord of all, who taught people temperance.

That, however, is enough on this point. What will they say to the other marvels of his divinity? At what man's death was the sun darkened and the earth shaken? Why, even to this day people are dying, and they did so also before that time. When did any such marvels happen in their case? Now shall we pass over the deeds done in his earthly body and mention those after his resurrection? Has any person's teaching, in any place or at any time, ever prevailed everywhere as one and the same, from one end of the earth to the other, so that his worship has fairly flown

---

1   Aesculapius – According to Greek mythology, the son of Apollo who became the god of healing.

through every land? Again, if, as they say, Christ is a man only and not God the Word, why do not the gods of the Greeks prevent his entering their domains? Or why, on the other hand, does the Word himself dwelling in our midst make an end of their worship by his teaching and put their fraud to shame?

§50 – Jesus Is Greater than Kings of the Earth

Many before him have been kings and tyrants of the earth; history tells also of many among the Chaldeans, Egyptians, and Indians who were wise men and magicians. But which of those, I do not say after his death, but while yet in this life, was ever able so far to prevail as to fill the whole world with his teaching and retrieve so great a multitude from the cowardly fear of idols as our Savior has won over from idols to himself? The Greek philosophers have compiled many works with persuasiveness and much skill in words; but what fruit have they to show for this such as has the cross of Christ? Their wise thoughts were persuasive enough until they died; yet even in their lifetime their seeming influence was counterbalanced by their rivalry with one another, for they were a jealous company and spoke against each other. But the Word of God, by strangest paradox, teaching in poorer language, has put the choicest sophists in the shade, and by confounding their teachings and drawing all people to himself he has filled his own assemblies. Moreover, and this is the marvelous thing, by going down as a man to death, he has confounded all the sounding utterances of the wise men about the idols. For whose death ever drove out demons, or whose death did ever demons fear, except that of Christ? For where the Savior is named, there every demon is driven out. Again, who has ever so rid people of their natural passions that fornicators become chaste and murderers no longer wield the sword and those who formerly were cowards become courageous? In a word, what persuaded the barbarians and pagans in every place to drop their madness and give heed to peace, except the faith of Christ and the sign of the cross? What other things have given people such certain faith in immortality as have the cross of Christ and the resurrection of his body? The Greeks told all sorts of false tales, but they could never pretend that their idols rose again from death: indeed, it never entered their heads that a body could exist again after death at all. And one would be particularly ready to listen to them on this point, because by these opinions they have exposed the weakness of their own idolatry, at the same time yielding to Christ the possibility of bodily resurrection, so that by that means he might be recognized by all as Son of God.

§51 – Who Else Could Bring Sexual Purity and End Warfare?

Again, who among humanity, either after death or while yet living, taught about virginity and did not account this virtue impossible for human beings? But Christ our Savior and King of all has so prevailed with his teaching on this subject that even children not yet of lawful age promise that virginity which transcends the law. And who among humanity has ever been able to penetrate even to Scythians and Ethiopians, or Parthians or Armenians or those who are said to live beyond Hyrcania, or even the Egyptians and Chaldeans, people who give heed to magic and are more than naturally enslaved by the fear of demons and cruel in their habits, and to preach at all about virtue and self-control and against the worshiping of idols, as has the Lord of all, the Power of God, our Lord Jesus Christ? Yet he not only preached through his own disciples, but also wrought so persuasively on human understanding that, laying aside their cruel habits and forsaking the worship of their ancestral gods, they learned to know him and through him to worship the Father. While they were yet idolaters, the Greeks and Barbarians were always at war with each other, and were even cruel to their own families. Nobody could travel by land or sea at all unless he was armed with swords because of their irreconcilable quarrels with each other. Indeed, the whole course of their life was carried on with weapons, and the sword with them replaced the staff and was the mainstay of all aid. All this time, as I said before, they were serving idols and offering sacrifices to demons, and for all the superstitious awe that accompanied this idol worship, nothing could wean them from that warlike spirit. But, strange to relate, since they came over to the school of Christ, as people moved with real compunction, they have laid aside their murderous cruelty and are war-minded no more. On the contrary, all is peace among them, and nothing remains except desire for friendship.

§52 – Who Else Could Turn Enemies into Friends?

Who, then, is he who has done these things and has united in peace those who hated each other, except the beloved Son of the Father, the common Savior of all, Jesus Christ, who by his own love underwent all things for our salvation? Even from the beginning, moreover, this peace that he was to administer was foretold, for Scripture says, "They shall beat their swords into plowshares, and their spears into pruning hooks; nation shall not lift up sword against nation, neither shall they learn war anymore" (Isa 2:4). Nor is this by any means incredible.

The barbarians of the present day are naturally cruel in their habits, and as long as they sacrifice to their idols they rage furiously against each other and cannot bear to be a single hour without weapons. But when they hear the teaching of Christ, immediately they turn from fighting to farming, and instead of arming themselves with swords extend their hands in prayer. In a word, instead of fighting each other, they take up arms against the devil and the demons, and overcome them by their sobriety and integrity of soul. These facts are proof of the divinity of the Savior, for he has taught people what they could never learn among the idols. It is also no small exposure of the weakness and nothingness of demons and idols, for it was because they knew their own weakness that the demons were always setting people to fight each other, fearing lest, if they ceased from mutual strife, they would turn to attack the demons themselves. For in truth the disciples of Christ, instead of fighting each other, stand arrayed against demons by their habits and virtuous actions, and chase them away and mock at their captain the devil. Even in youth they are sexually pure; they endure in times of testing and persevere in toils. When they are insulted, they are patient; when robbed, they make light of it; and, marvelous to relate, they make light even of death itself and become martyrs of Christ.

§53 – Who Else Could Accomplish So Much?

And here is another proof of the divinity of the Savior, which is indeed utterly amazing. What mere human—magician, tyrant, or king—was ever able by himself to do so much? Did anyone ever fight against the whole system of idol worship and the whole host of demons and all magic and all the wisdom of the Greeks, at a time when all of these were strong and flourishing and taking everybody in, as did our Lord, the very Word of God? Yet he is even now invisibly exposing every person's error and singlehandedly is carrying off all people from them all, so that those who used to worship idols now tread them under foot, reputed magicians burn their books, and the wise prefer to all studies the interpretation of the gospels. They are deserting those whom formerly they worshiped; they worship and confess as Christ and God him whom they used to ridicule as crucified. Their so-called gods are routed by the sign of the cross, and the crucified Savior is proclaimed in all the world as God and Son of God. Moreover, the gods worshiped among the Greeks are now falling into disrepute among them on account of the disgraceful things they did, for those who receive the teaching of Christ are more chaste in life than they. If these, and the like of them, are human works, let anyone who will show us similar ones done by people in former times, and so convince us. But if they are shown to be and are the works not of people but of God, why are the unbelievers so irreligious as not to recognize the Master who did them? They are afflicted as a person would be who failed to recognize God the Creator through the works of creation. For surely if they had recognized his divinity through his power over the universe, they would recognize also that the bodily works of Christ are not human, but are those of the Savior of all, the Word of God. And had they recognized this, as Paul says, "They would not have crucified the Lord of glory" (1 Cor 2:8).

§54 – The Savior's Achievements Are More than We Could Imagine

As, then, one who desires to see God who by nature is invisible and not to be beheld may yet perceive and know him through his works, so too let one who does not see Christ with their understanding at least consider him in his bodily works and test whether they be human or of God. If they be human, then let them scoff; but if they be of God, let them not mock at things which are no fit subject for scorn, but rather let them recognize the fact and marvel that things divine have been revealed to us by such humble means, that through death deathlessness has been made known to us, and through the incarnation of the Word, the Mind whence all things proceed has been declared, and its Agent and Ordainer, the Word of God himself. He, indeed, assumed humanity that we might become God.[2] He manifested himself by means of a body in order that we might perceive the mind of the unseen Father. He endured shame from humanity that we might inherit immortality. He himself was unhurt by this, for he is impassable and incorruptible; but by his own impassability he kept and healed those suffering on whose account he thus endured.

> *So many are the Savior's achievements that follow from his incarnation, that to try to number them is like gazing at the open sea and trying to count the waves.*

In short, such and so many are the Savior's achievements that follow from his incarnation, that to try to number them is like gazing at the open sea and trying to count the waves. One cannot see all the waves with one's eyes, for when one tries to do so those that are following on baffle

---

2 Athanasius does not mean humanity ceases to be human and becomes something equal to God. Rather, he is referring to the apex of salvation as joining in the communion of the Father, Son, and Holy Spirit. As 2 Peter 1:4 says, we will "become partakers of the divine nature."

one's senses. Even so, when one wants to take in all the achievements of Christ in the body, one cannot do so, even by reckoning them up, for the things that transcend one's thought are always more than those one thinks that one has grasped.

As we cannot speak adequately about even a part of his work, therefore, it will be better for us not to speak about it as a whole. So we will mention but one thing more, and then leave the whole for you to marvel at. For, indeed, everything about it is marvelous, and wherever people turn their gaze they see the divinity of the Word and are struck with awe.

§55 – Christ Triumphs over Idolatry, Greek Wisdom, and Magic

The substance of what we have said so far may be summarized as follows. Since the Savior came to dwell among us, not only does idolatry no longer increase, but it is getting less and gradually ceasing to be. Similarly, not only does the wisdom of the Greeks no longer make any progress, but that which used to be is disappearing. And demons, so far from continuing to impose on people by their deceits, oracles, and sorceries, are routed by the sign of the cross if they so much as try. On the other hand, while idolatry and everything else that opposes the faith of Christ is daily dwindling, weakening, and falling, see, the Savior's teaching is increasing everywhere! Worship, then, the Savior who "is above all" (John 3:31) and mighty, even God the Word, and condemn those who are being defeated and made to disappear by him. When the sun has come, darkness prevails no longer; any of it that may be left anywhere is driven away. So also, now that the divine epiphany of the Word of God has taken place, the darkness of idols prevails no more, and all parts of the world in every direction are enlightened by his teaching. Similarly, if a king be reigning somewhere, but stays in his own house and does not let himself be seen, it often happens that some insubordinate fellows, taking advantage of his retirement, will have themselves proclaimed in his stead; and each of them, being invested with the semblance of kingship, misleads the simple who, because they cannot enter the palace and see the real king, are led astray by just hearing a king named. When the real king emerges, however, and comes into view, things stand differently. The insubordinate impostors are shown up by his presence, and people, seeing the real king, forsake those who previously misled them. In the same way the demons used formerly to impose on people, investing themselves with the honor due to God. But since the Word of God has been manifested in a body, and has made known to us his own Father, the fraud of the demons is stopped and made to disappear; and people, turning their eyes to the true God, Word of the Father, forsake the idols and come to know the true God.

Now this is proof that Christ is God, the Word and Power of God. For whereas human things cease and the fact of Christ remains, it is clear to all that the things which cease are temporary, but that he who remains is God and very Son of God, the solely begotten Word.

Discussion Questions

 What are some concerns or criticisms of the message of Jesus in our society today?

 In your faith journey, have you been able to wrestle honestly with questions and doubts? How can acknowledging valid questions be a healthy part of our faith?

 Do you think most people's resistances to Christianity are primarily intellectual? Or are there other factors at play of which Christians should be aware?

 What is one way you can seek to understand the perspective of unbelievers in your community?

 What relationships or rhythms in your life enable you to regularly engage with unbelievers in meaningful ways?

Chapter 8
Living to the Glory of God

While Athanasius has provided a brief introduction to Christianity, he hopes readers will continue to plumb the depths of truth through the study of Scripture. Furthermore, although Athanasius has focused primarily on the first coming of Christ, we also ought to look to the second coming of Christ. In between, we need Christian virtue to guide the mind toward truth in Christ. All of this is to the glory of the triune God.

***

§56 – The First and Second Comings of Christ

Here then, O blessed one, is our offering to you who love Christ, a brief statement of the faith of Christ and of the manifestation of his divinity to us. This will give you a beginning, and you must go on to prove its truth by the study of the Scriptures. They were written and inspired by God; and we, who have learned from inspired teachers who read the Scriptures and became martyrs for the divinity of Christ, make further contribution to your eagerness to learn. From the Scriptures you will learn also of his second manifestation to us, glorious and divine indeed, when he shall come not in lowliness but in his proper glory, no longer in humiliation but in majesty, no longer to suffer but to bestow on us all the fruit of his cross—the resurrection and incorruptibility. No longer will he then be judged, but rather will himself be Judge, judging each and all according to their deeds done in the body, whether good or bad. Then for the good is laid up the heavenly kingdom, but for those that practice evil, outer darkness and the eternal fire. So also the Lord himself says, "But I tell you, from now on you will see the Son of Man seated at the right hand of Power and coming on the clouds of heaven" (Matt 26:64). For that day we have one of his own sayings to prepare us, "Stay awake, for you do not know on what day your Lord is coming" (Matt 24:42). And blessed Paul says, "we must all appear before the judgment seat of Christ, so that each one may receive what is due for what he has done in the body, whether good or evil" (2 Cor 5:10).

§57 – Christian Virtue Must Guide the Mind

But for the searching and right understanding of the Scriptures there is need of a good life and a pure soul, and for Christian virtue to guide the mind to grasp, so far as human nature can, the truth concerning God the Word. One cannot possibly understand the teaching of the saints unless one has a pure mind and is trying to imitate their life. Anyone who wants to look at sunlight naturally wipes his eye clear first, in order to make, at any rate, some approximation to the purity of that on which he looks;

and a person wishing to see a city or country goes to the place in order to do so. Similarly, anyone who wishes to understand the mind of the sacred writers must first cleanse their own life and approach the saints by copying their deeds. Thus united to them in the fellowship of life, one will both understand the things revealed to them by God and, then escaping the peril that threatens sinners in the judgment, will receive that which is laid up for the saints in the kingdom of heaven. Of that reward it is written, "No eye has seen, nor ear heard, nor the heart of man imagined, what God has prepared" (1 Cor 2:9) for them that live a godly life and love the God and Father in Christ Jesus our Lord, through whom and with whom be to the Father himself, with the Son himself, in the Holy Spirit, honor and might and glory to ages of ages. Amen.

Discussion Questions

Athanasius positions the Christian life in between the first and second comings of Christ. How does the fact that Christ has already come but has not yet returned shape our expectations for life today?

Athanasius argues that vice and virtue shape our beliefs. Can you think of any examples of how a vice or virtue impacts someone's thinking?

The Bible ends with the exclamation, "Come, Lord Jesus!" (Rev 22:20). What aspects of life today (or of the hope of life in eternity) make your heart long for the return of Christ?

Read Revelation 22:1–4 and 2 Corinthians 5:17. How can our lives today be a glimpse of the new creation to come?

How has the consistent reading of Scripture deepened your relationship with God? If you have never experienced consistency in reading Scripture, how might you create rhythms in your life to make this a reality?

Appendix 1
The Life of Antony[1]

The Life of Antony is *a biography by Athanasius about a well-known Christian who vastly shaped the monastic movement* in the early church. However, more than a mere biography, this retelling of Antony's story is a way for Athanasius to portray the model Christian life. It is Athanasius's theology in the form of an embodied narrative. And while Athanasius sees God renewing all of creation through his Son, he also sees the Christian life as one of renewal in Christ—a renewal that comes through struggle and surrender.*

The Christian life for Athanasius, as exemplified through Antony, is one of self-denial, simplicity, discipline, and spiritual warfare. While solitude is a key part of Antony's

---

[1] The full title is *The Life and Affairs of Our Holy Father Antony (Written and Dispatched to the Monks Abroad)*. What follows is a portion of *The Life of Antony*. To read the work in its entirety, see Athanasius, *The Life of Antony and the Letter to Marcellinus*, trans. Robert C. Gregg, Classics of Western Spirituality (Mahwah, NJ: Paulist, 1980) or go to newadvent.org/fathers/2811.htm.

story, and certainly what he is most known for, his solitude was not an end in and of itself and was different than what people often assume. Going into the wilderness alone, for Antony, was not escapism from the world, nor was it a rejection of community. Solitude was Antony's way of seeking purity through discipline for the sake of building others up. For example, while Antony did spend much time alone, he also had a constant stream of visitors, maintained lasting relationships, and consistently emerged to teach others that which he was learning in solitude. In other words, although Antony was often isolated geographically, he was rarely disconnected socially. Furthermore, Antony's solitude was far from peaceful and serene. Along with working (weaving baskets), he spent much of his time fighting temptation and battling demons. For Antony, life in the wilderness was less about serenity and more about spiritual warfare, discipline, fasting, and intense prayer.

Athanasius's biography of Antony was widely read in the ancient world and immensely impacted individuals and communities. Gregory of Nazianzus described The Life of Antony *as a rule of life in the form of a narrative.*[2] *In other words, it gave a blueprint for communities about how to live the Christian life together. Perhaps* The Life of Antony's *greatest impact is the part it played in Augustine of Hippo's*[3] *conversion and its shaping of his sense of the Christian life.*

***

---

2   See Hank Voss, "Soul Work and Soul Care: Learning to Be Intentional about Our 'Rule of Life,'" in Benedict of Nursia and Basil of Caesarea, *Becoming a Community of Disciples: Guidelines from Abbot Benedict and Bishop Basil*, ed. Greg Peters, Sacred Roots Spiritual Classics 2 (Upland, IN: Samuel Morris Publications, 2021), 121–41.

3   Augustine of Hippo (AD 354–430) – The Bishop of Hippo who would go on to be one of the most influential theologians in all of history.

Outline

- §§1–4: Antony Becomes a Monk
- §§5–15: Early Years of Monasticism
- §§16–43: Antony's Teaching
- §§44–86: Later Years of Ministry
- §§87–94: Death and Legacy

§1 – Antony's Childhood

Antony, you must know, was by descent an Egyptian: his parents were from a good family and possessed considerable wealth, and as they were Christians, he also was raised in the same faith. In infancy he was brought up with his parents, knowing nothing else but them and his home. But when he arrived at boyhood and was advancing in years, he could not endure to learn letters, not caring to associate with other boys; but all his desire was, as it is written of Jacob, to live a plain life at home (Gen 25:27). With his parents he used to attend the Lord's house, and neither as a child was he idle nor when older did he despise his parents; but he was both obedient to his father and mother and attentive to what was read, keeping in his heart what was profitable in what he heard. And though as a child brought up in moderate affluence, he did not trouble his parents for varied or luxurious food, nor was this a source of pleasure to him; but he was content simply with what he found and sought nothing further.

§2 – Antony Sells His Possessions and Gives to the Poor

After the death of his father and mother, he was left alone with one little sister: his age was about eighteen or twenty, and on him the care both of home and sister rested. Now it was not six months after the death of his parents when, going according to custom into the Lord's house, he gathered his thoughts and reflected as he walked how the apostles left all and followed the Savior (Matt 4:20); and how they in the book of Acts sold their possessions and brought and laid them at the apostles' feet for distribution to the needy (Acts 4:35), and what and how great a hope was laid up for them in heaven. Pondering over these things he entered the church, and it happened the Gospel was being read, and he heard the Lord saying to the rich man, "If you would be perfect, go, sell what you possess and give to the poor, and you will have treasure in heaven" (Matt 19:21). Antony, as though God had put him in mind of the saints, and the passage had been read on his account, went out immediately from the church, and gave the possessions of his forefathers to the villagers—they were three hundred acres, fertile and beautiful—so that they should not disturb him and his sister. And all the rest that was movable he sold, and having got together much money he gave it to the poor, reserving a little however for his sister's sake.

§3 – The Beginning of Monastic Discipline

And again as he went into the church, hearing the Lord say in the Gospel, "Therefore do not be anxious about tomorrow" (Matt 6:34), he could stay no longer, but went out and gave those things also to the poor. Having committed his sister to known and faithful virgins,[4] and put her into a convent to be brought up, he then devoted himself outside his house to discipline, paying attention

---

4   Virgins – Single Christian women who decided to devote themselves fully to pursuing Christ.

to his soul, and training himself with patience. For there were not yet so many monasteries in Egypt, and no monk at all knew of the distant desert; but all who wished to pay attention to their souls practiced the discipline in solitude near their own village.[5] Now there was then in the next village an old man who had lived the life of a hermit from his youth up. Antony, after he had seen this man, imitated him in godliness. And at first, he began to abide in places outside the village: then if he heard of a good man anywhere, like a prudent bee, he went forth and sought him, nor turned back to his own palace until he had seen him; and he returned, having got from the good man, as it were, supplies for his journey in the way of virtue. So dwelling there at first, he confirmed his purpose not to return to the home of his fathers nor to the remembrance of his family, but to keep all his desire and energy for perfecting his discipline. He worked, however, with his hands, having heard, "If anyone is not willing to work, let him not eat" (2 Thess 3:10), and part he spent on bread and part he gave to the needy. And he was constant in prayer, knowing that one ought to pray in secret unceasingly (Matt 6:7; 1 Thess 5:17). For he had listened so carefully to what was read that none of the things that were written fell from him to the ground, but he remembered all, and afterward his memory served him like books.

§4 – Learning from Many Teachers

Conducting himself in this way, Antony was beloved by all. He subjected himself in sincerity to the good men whom he visited and learned thoroughly where each surpassed

---

[5] If you are interested in learning more about the discipleship practices of monks, see Greg Peters, *The Monkhood of All Believers: The Monastic Foundation of Christian Spirituality* (Grand Rapids: Baker Academic, 2018).

him in zeal and discipline. He observed the graciousness of one, the unceasing prayer of another; he took knowledge of one's freedom from anger, and another's loving-kindness; he paid attention to one as he watched,[6] to another as he studied; one he admired for his endurance, another for his fasting and sleeping on the ground; the meekness of one and the long-suffering of another he watched with care, while he took note of the reverence toward Christ and the mutual love which animated all. Thus filled, he returned to his own place of discipline and from then on would strive to unite the qualities of each, eager to show in himself the virtues of all. With others of the same age he had no rivalry except this only: that he should not be second to them in higher things. And he did this not to hurt the feelings of others, but for them to rejoice over him. So all the people of that village and the good men in whose intimacy he was, when they saw that he was a man of this sort, used to call him God-beloved. And some welcomed him as a son, others as a brother.

He took note of the reverence toward Christ and the mutual love which animated all.

---

§5 – Opposition from the Enemy Begins

But the devil, who hates and envies what is good, could not endure to see such a resolution in a youth, but began to carry out against him what he had worked against others. First of all he tried to lead him away from the discipline,

---

6 Watching – The ancient practice that consists of an individual rising in the middle of the night to spend time in focused prayer. The tradition is rooted in Luke's account of Jesus praying during the night (Luke 6:12–13).

whispering to him the remembrance of his wealth, care for his sister, claims of family, love of money, love of glory, the various pleasures of the table and the other relaxations of life, and at last the difficulty of virtue and the labor of it; he suggested also the weakness of the body and the length of the time. In a word, he raised in his mind a great dust of debate, wishing to ban him from his settled purpose. But when the enemy saw himself to be too weak for Antony's determination and that he rather was conquered by the other's firmness, overthrown by his great faith and falling through his constant prayers, then at length putting his trust in the weapons which are "in the muscles of his belly" (Job 40:16)[7] and boasting in them—for they are his first snare for the young—he attacked the young man, disturbing him by night and harassing him by day, so that even the onlookers saw the struggle which was going on between them. The one would suggest foul thoughts, and the other counter them with prayers; the one fire him with lust, the other, as one who seemed to blush, fortify his body with faith, prayers, and fasting. And the devil, the unhappy being, one night even took upon him the shape of a woman and imitated all her acts simply to tempt Antony. But he, his mind filled with Christ and the nobility inspired by him, and considering the spirituality of the soul, quenched the coal of the other's deceit. Again, the enemy suggested the ease of pleasure. But he, like a man filled with rage and grief, turned his thoughts to the threatened fire and the gnawing worm, and setting these in array against his adversary, passed through the temptation unscathed. All this was a source of shame to his foe. For he, deeming himself like God, was now mocked by a

---

7 Athanasisus assumes the descriptions of Behemoth and Leviathan in this passage refer to Satan.

young man, and he who boasted himself against flesh and blood was being put to flight by a man in the flesh. For the Lord was working with Antony—the Lord who for our sake took flesh and gave the body victory over the devil, so that all who truly fight can say, "though it was not I, but the grace of God that is with me" (1 Cor 15:10).

§6 – Ongoing Struggle against the Devil

At last, when the dragon still could not overthrow Antony but saw himself thrust out of his heart, gnashing his teeth as it is written, and as it were beside himself, he appeared to Antony like a dark figure, taking a visible shape in accordance with the color of his mind. And cringing to him, as it were, he attacked him with thoughts no longer, for cunning as he was, he had been defeated, but at last spoke in a human voice and said, "Many I deceived, many I cast down; but now attacking you and your labors as I had many others, I proved weak." When Antony asked, "Who are you who speaks with me?" he answered with a lamentable voice, "I am the friend of whoredom, and have taken upon me incitements which lead to it against the young. I am called the spirit of lust. How many have I deceived who wished to live soberly, how many are the pure whom by my incitements I have overpersuaded! I am he on account of whom also the prophet reproves those who have fallen, saying, 'For a spirit of whoredom has led them astray' (Hos 4:12). For by me they have been tripped up. I am he who has so often troubled you and has so often been overthrown by you." But Antony, having given thanks to the Lord, with good courage said to him, "You are very despicable then, for you are dark-hearted and weak as a child. From now on I shall have no trouble from you: 'The Lord is on my side as my helper; I shall look in triumph on those who hate me'" (Ps 118:7). Having heard this, the shadowy one straightway fled, shuddering at the words and dreading any longer even to come near the man.

§7 – A Life of Discipline

This was Antony's first struggle against the devil, or rather this victory was the Savior's work in Antony: "He condemned sin in the flesh, in order that the righteous requirement of the law might be fulfilled in us, who walk not according to the flesh but according to the Spirit" (Rom 8:3–4). But neither did Antony, although the evil one had fallen, afterward relax his care and despise him; nor did the enemy, as though conquered, cease to lay snares for him. For again he went around as a lion seeking some occasion against him. But Antony, having learned from the Scriptures that the devices of the devil are many, zealously continued the discipline, reckoning that though the devil had not been able to deceive his heart by bodily pleasure (Eph 6:11), he would try to ensnare him by other means. For the demon loves sin. So more and more he denied the body and kept it in subjection, lest happily having conquered on one side, he should be dragged down on the other (1 Cor 9:27). He therefore planned to accustom himself to a more severe mode of life. And many marveled, but he himself used to bear the work easily; for the eagerness of soul, through the length of time it had dwelt in him, had resulted in a good habit in him, so that taking but little initiation from others he showed great zeal in this matter. He kept watch* to such an extent that he often continued the whole night without sleep; and this not once but often, to the marvel of others. He ate once a day, after sunset, sometimes once in two days, and often even only once in four. His food was bread and salt; his drink, water only.

Of meat and wine it is unnecessary even to speak, since no such thing was found with the other earnest men. A mat served him to sleep upon, but for the most part he lay upon the bare ground. He would not anoint himself with oil, saying it is good for the young to be earnest in training and not to seek what would exhaust the body; but they must accustom it to labor, mindful of the apostle's words, "For when I am weak, then I am strong" (2 Cor 12:10). "For," he said, "the fiber of the soul is then sound when the pleasures of the body are diminished." And he had come to this truly wonderful conclusion, "that progress in virtue, and retirement from the world for the sake of it, ought not to be measured by time, but by desire and permanence of purpose." He at least gave no thought to the past, but day by day, as if he were at the beginning of his discipline, applied greater pains for advancement, often repeating to himself the saying of Paul, "Forgetting what lies behind and straining forward to what lies ahead" (Phil 3:13). He was also mindful of the words spoken by the prophet Elijah, "As the Lord of hosts lives, before whom I stand" (1 Kgs 18:15). For he observed that in saying "today" the prophet did not consider the time that had gone by: but daily, as though ever beginning, he eagerly worked to make himself fit to appear before God, being pure in heart and ever ready to submit to his counsel and to him alone. And he used to say to himself that from the life of the great Elijah the ascetic* ought to see his own as in a mirror.

§8 – Seeking Solitude

Thus tightening his hold upon himself, Antony departed to the tombs, which happened to be at a distance from the village; and having told one of his friends to bring him bread at intervals of many days, he entered one of the tombs, and the other having shut the door on him, he remained within alone. And when the enemy could not endure it, but was even fearful that in a short time Antony would fill the desert with the discipline, coming one night with a multitude of demons, he so cut him with stripes that he lay on the ground speechless from the excessive pain. For he affirmed that the torture had been so excessive that no blows inflicted by a person could ever have caused him such torment. But by the providence of God—for the Lord never overlooks them that hope in him—the next day his friend came bringing him the loaves. And having opened the door and seeing him lying on the ground as though dead, he lifted him up and carried him to the church in the village, and laid him upon the ground. And many of his family and the villagers sat around Antony as around a corpse. But about midnight he came to himself and arose, and when he saw them all asleep and his friend alone watching,* he motioned with his head for him to approach, and asked him to carry him again to the tombs without waking anybody.

§9 – Under Attack but Faithful

He was carried therefore by the man, and as was his practice, when the door was shut, he was within alone. And he could not stand up on account of the blows, but he prayed as he lay. And after he had prayed, he said with a shout, "Here am I, Antony; I flee not from your beatings, for even if you inflict more, nothing shall separate me from the love of Christ" (Rom 8:35). And then he sang, "Though an army encamp against me, my heart shall not fear" (Ps 27:3). These were the thoughts and words of this ascetic.* But the enemy, who hates good, marveling that after the blows he dared to return, called together his hounds and burst forth,

"You see," he said, "that neither by the spirit of lust nor by blows did we stop the man, but that he braves us; let us attack him in another fashion." Now changes of form for evil are easy for the devil, so in the night they made such a noise that the whole of that place seemed to be shaken by an earthquake, and the demons as if breaking the four walls of the dwelling seemed to enter through them, coming in the likeness of beasts and creeping things. And the place was suddenly filled with the forms of lions, bears, leopards, bulls, serpents, snakes, scorpions, and wolves, and each of them was moving according to his nature. The lion was roaring, wishing to attack, the bull seeming to toss with its horns, the serpent creeping but unable to approach, and the wolf as it rushed on was restrained; altogether the noises of the creatures, with their angry ragings, were dreadful. But Antony, stricken and provoked by them, felt bodily pains more severe still. He lay watching,* however, with unshaken soul, groaning from bodily anguish; but his mind was clear, and, as in mockery, he said, "If there had been any power in you, it would have been enough had one of you come, but since the Lord has made you weak, you attempt to terrify me by numbers: and a proof of your weakness is that you take the shapes of brute beasts." And again, with boldness he said, "If you are able, and have received power against me, delay not to attack; but if you are unable, why trouble me uselessly? For faith in our Lord is a seal and a wall of safety to us." So after many attempts they gnashed their teeth upon him, because they were mocking themselves rather than him.

§10 – Delivered by the Lord

Nor was the Lord then forgetful of Antony's wrestling, but was at hand to help him. So looking up he saw the roof, as it were, opened, and a ray of light descending to him. The demons suddenly vanished, the pain of his body immediately ceased, and the building was again whole. But Antony, feeling the help, getting his breath again, and being freed from pain, asked the vision which had appeared to him, "Where were you? Why did you not appear at the beginning to stop my pains?" And a voice came to him, "Antony, I was here, but I waited to see you fight; and since you have endured, and have not been defeated, I will ever be a comfort to you, and will make your name known everywhere." Having heard this, Antony arose and prayed, and received such strength that he perceived that he had more power in his body than formerly. And he was then about thirty-five years old.

§11 – Seeking Community

And on the following day he went forth still more eagerly bent on the service of God, and having fallen in with the old man he had met previously, he asked him to dwell with him in the desert. But when the other declined on account of his great age, and because as yet there was no such custom, Antony himself set off immediately to the mountain. And yet again the enemy, seeing his zeal and wishing to stop it, cast in his way what seemed to be a great silver dish. But Antony, seeing the deceit of the evil one, stood, and having looked at the dish, he put the devil in it to shame, saying, "Where does a dish come from in the desert? This road is not well-worn, nor is there here a trace of any traveler; it could not have fallen without being missed on account of its size; and he who had lost it having turned back, to seek it, would have found it, for it is a desert place. This is some trick of the devil. Oh, you evil one, not with this will you stop my purpose; let it go with you to destruction." And when Antony had said this it vanished like smoke from the face of fire.

§12 – Alone in the Mountain

Then again as he went on he saw what was this time not visionary, but real gold scattered in the way. But whether the devil showed it, or some better power to test the athlete and show the evil one that Antony truly did not care for money, he did not tell nor do we know. But it is certain that what appeared was gold. And Antony marveled at the quantity, but passed by it as though he were going over fire; so he did not even turn, but hurried on at a run to lose sight of the place. More and more confirmed in his purpose, he hurried to the mountain, and having found a fort, so long deserted that it was full of creeping things, on the other side of the river, he crossed over to it and lived there. The reptiles, as though someone were chasing them, immediately left the place. But he built up the entrance completely, having stored up loaves for six months—this is a custom of the Thebans,[8] and the loaves often remain fresh a whole year—and, as he found water within, he descended as into a holy place and lived within by himself, never going out nor looking at anyone who came. Thus, he spent a long time training himself and received loaves, let down from above, twice a year.

§13 – A Visit from Friends

But those of his friends who came, since he did not permit them to enter, often used to spend days and nights outside, and heard as it were crowds within talking, clattering, sending forth pitiful voices and crying, "Go from what is

---

8   Thebans – People from the city of Thebes, the ancient capital of Upper Egypt.

He saw what was this time not visionary, but real gold scattered in the way.

ours. What are you even doing in the desert? You cannot stand our attack." So at first those outside thought there were some men fighting with him, and that they had entered by ladders; but when stooping down they saw through a hole there was nobody, they were afraid, deciding they were demons, and they called on Antony. He quickly heard them, though he had not given a thought to the demons, and coming to the door he asked them to leave and not to be afraid, "Because," he said, "the demons make their seeming onslaughts against those who are cowardly. Sign yourselves therefore with the cross, and leave boldly, and let these entertain themselves." So they left fortified with the sign of the cross. But he remained in no way harmed by the evil spirits, nor was he wearied with the contest, for there came to his aid visions from above, and the weakness of the foe relieved him of much trouble and armed him with greater zeal. For his friends used often to come expecting to find him dead, and would hear him singing, "God shall arise, his enemies shall be scattered; and those who hate him shall flee before him! As smoke is driven away, so you shall drive them away; as wax melts before fire, so the wicked shall perish before God!" (Ps 68:1–2), and again, "All nations surrounded me; in the name of the Lord, I cut them off!" (Ps 118:10).

§14 – After Twenty Years of Solitude, Antony Ministers to Many

And so for nearly twenty years he continued training himself in solitude, never going forth, and but seldom seen by any. After this, when many were eager and wishful to imitate his discipline, and his friends came and began to cast down and tear off the door by force, Antony, as from a holy place, came forth initiated in the mysteries and filled with the Spirit of God. Then for the first time he was seen outside of the fort by those who came to see him. And they, when they saw him, wondered at the sight, for he had the same bodily condition as before, and was neither fat, like a person without exercise, nor lean from fasting and striving with the demons, but he was just the same as they had known him before his season of solitude. And again, his soul was free from blemish, for it was neither contracted as if by grief, nor relaxed by pleasure, nor possessed by laughter or dejection, for he was not troubled when he saw

---

But he was altogether grounded as being guided by reason and abiding in a natural state.

---

the crowd nor overjoyed at being saluted by so many. But he was altogether grounded as being guided by reason and abiding in a natural state. Through him the Lord healed the bodily sicknesses of many present and cleansed others from evil spirits. And he gave grace to Antony in speaking, so that he comforted many that were sorrowful and set those with disagreements into unity, exhorting all to prefer the love of Christ before all that is in the world. And while he exhorted and advised them to remember the good things to come, and the loving-kindness of God toward us, "He who did not spare his own Son but gave him up for us all" (Rom 8:32), he persuaded many to embrace a life of solitude. And thus, it happened in the end that monasteries arose even in the mountains, and the desert was populated by monks, who came forth from their own people and enrolled themselves for citizenship in the heavens.

§15 – The Father of a Movement

But when he was obliged to cross the Arsenoitic Canal[9]—and the occasion of it was the visitation of the sisters and brothers—the canal was full of crocodiles. And by simply praying, he entered it, and all of them with him, and passed over in safety. And having returned to his monastery, he applied himself to the same noble and courageous exercises; and by frequent conversation he increased the eagerness of those already monks, stirred up in most of the rest the love of the discipline, and speedily by the attraction of his words monasteries multiplied, and he directed them all as a father.

§87 – Summary of Antony's Holistic Ministry

Thus, therefore, he warned the cruel. But the rest who came to him he taught in such a way that they immediately forgot their lawsuits, and he blessed those who left the ways of the world. And he supported those who were wronged in such a way that you would imagine that he, and not the others, was the sufferer.[10] Further, he was able to be of such use to all that many soldiers and people who had great possessions laid aside the burdens of life and became monks for the rest of their days. And it was as if a physician had been given by God to Egypt. For who in grief met Antony and did not return rejoicing? Who came mourning for his dead and did not immediately put off his sorrow? Who came in anger and was not converted to friendship? What poor and low-spirited man met him who,

---

9 Arsenoitic Canal – A canal connecting the Nile River and the Faiyum Oasis.

10 For more on this theme, see John Woolman, *Mission with Prophetic Power: The Journal of John Woolman*, ed. Evan B. Howard, Sacred Roots Spiritual Classics 12 (Upland, IN: Samuel Morris Publications, 2023).

hearing him and looking upon him, did not despise wealth and console himself in his poverty? What monk, having being neglectful, came to him and became not all the stronger? What young man, having come to the mountain and seen Antony, did not then deny himself pleasure and love temperance? Who, when tempted by a demon, came to him and did not find rest? And who came troubled with doubts and did not get peace of mind?

§89 – Antony Nears Death

It is worthwhile that I should relate, and that you, as you wish it, should hear, what his death was like. For this end of his is worthy of imitation.

According to his custom, he visited the monks in the outer mountain and, having learned from providence that his own end was at hand, he said to the sisters and brothers, "This is my last visit to you which I shall make. And I shall be surprised if we see each other again in this life. At length the time of my departure is at hand, for I am nearly one hundred and five years old." And when they heard it they wept, and embraced and kissed the old man. But he, as though sailing from a foreign city to his own, spoke joyously and exhorted them, "Not to grow idle in their labors, nor to become faint in their training, but to live as though dying daily (Luke 9:23). And as he had said before, zealously to guard the soul from repulsive thoughts, eagerly to imitate the saints, and to have nothing to do with the Meletian[11] schismatics, for you know their wicked and profane character. Nor have any fellowship

---

11 Meletians – A group that broke away from the church of Alexandria over the issue of how to respond to lapsed Christians who desired to return to the church. The Meletians opposed Athanasius when he first became bishop of Alexandria.

with the Arians,[12] for their ungodliness is clear to all. Nor be disturbed if you see the judges protect them, for it shall cease, and their seeming success is temporary and of short duration. Therefore, keep yourselves all the more untainted by them and observe the traditions of the fathers, and chiefly the holy faith in our Lord Jesus Christ, which you have learned from the Scripture and of which you have often been reminded by me."

§91 – Antony's Last Words

But he, knowing the custom,[13] and fearing that his body would be treated this way, hurried and, having said farewell to the monks in the outer mountain, entered the inner mountain where he was accustomed to live. And after a few months, he fell sick. Having summoned those who were there—there were two in number who had remained in the mountain fifteen years, practicing the discipline and attending on Antony on account of his age—he said to them, "I, as it is written, go the way of the fathers, for I perceive that I am called by the Lord (Josh 23:14). Be watchful and do not destroy your long discipline, but as though now making a beginning, zealously preserve your determination. For you know the treachery of the demons, how fierce they are, but how little power they have. Therefore, fear them not, but rather ever breathe Christ, and trust him. Live as though dying daily (Luke 9:23). Watch yourselves carefully and remember the admonition you have heard from me. Have

---

12 Arians – People who followed the teachings of Arius: namely, that Jesus had not eternally existed as God.

13 A custom developed in early monastic communities of preserving the bodies of revered monks in order to be displayed as relics for veneration by others. While this had become a common practice in the early church, Antony wanted to be remembered by his spiritual legacy, not his physical remains.

no fellowship with the schismatics, nor any dealings at all with the heretical Arians.* For you know how I shunned them on account of their hostility to Christ, and the strange doctrines of their heresy. Therefore, be the more earnest always to be followers first of God and then of the saints, that after death they also may receive you as well-known friends into the eternal dwelling (Heb 12:1–3). Ponder over these things and think of them, and if you have any care for me and are mindful of me as of a father, do not let anyone take my body into Egypt, lest they place me in the houses, for to avoid this I entered into the mountain and came here. Moreover, you know how I always rebuked those who had this custom and exhorted them to cease from it. Bury my body, therefore, and hide it underground yourselves, and let my words be observed by you that no one may know the place but you alone. For at the resurrection of the dead I shall receive my incorruptible body from the Savior. And divide my garments. To Athanasius the bishop give one sheepskin and the garment on which I am laid, that he himself gave me new, but which has grown old with me. To Serapion the bishop[14] give the other sheepskin, and keep the hair garment yourselves. For the rest, farewell my children, for Antony is departing, and is with you no more."

§92 – Antony's Death

Having said this, when they had kissed him, he lifted up his feet and, as though he saw friends coming to him and was glad because of them—for as he lay, his face appeared joyful—he died and was gathered to the fathers. And they afterward, according to his commandment, wrapped him

---

14 Serapion of Thmuis – A disciple of Antony and companion of Athanasius. Athanasius wrote Serapion three letters about the Holy Spirit. See Athanasius, "Letters to Serapion on the Holy Spirit."

up and buried him, hiding his body underground. And no one knows to this day where it was buried, except those two only. But each of those who received the sheepskin of the blessed Antony and the garment worn by him guards it as a precious treasure. For even to look on them is as it were to see Antony; and he who is clothed in them seems with joy to bear his teachings.

§93 – The Legacy of Antony

This is the end of Antony's life in the body and the above was the beginning of the discipline. Even if this account is small compared with his merit, still from this reflect how great Antony, the man of God, was. Who from his youth to so great an age preserved a uniform zeal for the discipline, and neither through old age was subdued by the desire of costly food, nor through the weakness of his body changed the fashion of his clothing, nor washed even his feet with water, and yet remained entirely free from harm? For his eyes were undimmed and quite sound, and he saw clearly; of his teeth he had not lost one, but they had become worn to the gums through the great age of the old man. He remained strong both in hands and feet; and while all men were using various foods, washings, and various garments, he appeared more cheerful and of greater strength. And the fact that his fame has been blazoned everywhere, that all regard him with wonder, and that those who have never seen him long for him, is clear proof of his virtue and God's love of his soul. For not from writings, nor from worldly wisdom, nor through any art was Antony renowned, but solely from his reverence toward God. That this was the gift of God no one will deny. For how into Spain and Gaul, into Rome and Africa, was the man heard of who lived hidden in a mountain, unless it was God who made his own known everywhere, who also promised this to Antony at the beginning? For even if they work secretly, even if they wish to remain in obscurity, yet the Lord shows them as lamps to lighten all, that those who hear may thus know that the commandments of God are able to make people prosper and thus be zealous in the path of virtue.

§94 – A Plea to Follow Antony's Example

Read these words, therefore, to the rest of the sisters and brothers that they may learn what the life of monks ought to be and may believe that our Lord and Savior Jesus Christ glorifies those who glorify him and leads those who serve him unto the end, not only to the kingdom of heaven, but here also. Even though they hide themselves and desire to withdraw from the world, he makes them illustrious and well-known everywhere on account of their virtue and the help they give others. And if need be, read this among those who do not believe, that even in this way they may learn that our Lord Jesus Christ is not only God and the Son of God, but also that the Christians who truly serve him and faithfully believe in him prove not only that the demons, whom the Greeks themselves think to be gods, are no gods, but also tread them under foot and put them to flight as deceivers and corrupters of humanity through Jesus Christ our Lord, to whom be glory forever and ever. Amen.

Discussion Questions

 What stood out to you from Antony's life as a Christian? How could you incorporate some of what you learned into your life today?

 What do you think is the proper balance of solitude and community? How can the life of Jesus offer guidance in this regard?

 What does Antony's life teach us about the role of spiritual warfare in the Christian life? Have you experienced temptation or attack from the enemy? If so, how did you respond?

 Read Psalm 46:10. What is difficult about being still before God?

 How can you incorporate times of solitude into your life?

Appendix 2
On the Psalms[1]

For Athanasius, reading Scripture is an essential aspect of the Christian life. And while all Scripture is inspired by God and necessary for training in righteousness (2 Tim 3:16), the Psalms are especially significant in the day-to-day lives of believers.

This is a letter written by Athanasius to a Christian who is suffering from an illness and wants to know how to better understand the Psalms. Athanasius writes with a pastoral voice, discussing how to approach the Psalms and arguing for their importance in the Christian life.

Athanasius makes three crucial arguments about the Psalms: (1) the Psalms are a microcosm of the whole Bible; (2) there is a

---

1   The full title is *A Letter of Athanasius, Our Holy Father, Archbishop of Alexandria, to Marcellinus on the Interpretation of the Psalms.* What follows below is a portion of Athanasius's *On the Psalms*. This appendix is reprinted for Athanasius of Alexandria,, *Letter to Marcellinus on the Psalms: Spiritual Wisdom from Today*, trans. Joel C. Elowsky (New Haven, CT: ICCS Press, 2021).

psalm for every season, circumstance, or emotion in life; and (3) the Psalms ultimately point forward to Jesus as the Messiah.

***

Outline

- §§1–2: The Psalms' Place within the Bible
- §§3–9: The Psalms as a Microcosm of Scripture
- §§10–13: The Psalms and the Rest of Scripture
- §§14–26: A Psalm for Every Occasion
- §§27–33: Misunderstandings of the Psalms

§1 – All Scripture Is Necessary for the Christian Life, Especially the Psalms

I am amazed at your resolve in Christ, beloved Marcellinus. For both in terms of your present trial, and indeed the many things you have endured in it, you have borne them well—and without neglecting the ascesis.[2] For learning from the bearer of your letter how you are managing with your ongoing illness, I found out that while you have had leisure to look at the entire divine Scripture, you have focused in on the most excellent book of the Psalms, and that you are eager to get at the meaning that is in each psalm. And for this reason, above all else, I approve of what you're doing since I have fallen in love with this book as well, even as I have with all the Scripture. In fact, I once had a conversation with a certain learned old man who had devoted a great deal to the study of the Psalter. And so I

---

2   Ascesis – Disciplined spiritual training or self-denial aimed at achieving greater holiness, purity, and union with God. The Greek word is based on the idea of athletic training which Christians appropriated for disciplining both body and soul..

also want to write to you to let you know how he explained it to me. For there was a certain grace and persuasiveness with his eloquent tale. This is what he said:

§2 – The Psalms Are a Microcosm of the Whole Bible

Everything that is in our Scripture, my child, is both old and new. It is God-breathed and profitable for teaching, as it is written (2 Tim 3:16). But the book of Psalms has, in addition, a certain persuasive observation for those who devote themselves to it. Now each book of Scripture serves its own purpose in what it relates, such as the Pentateuch telling of the birth of the world and the deeds of the patriarchs; of the exodus of Israel from Egypt, and the giving of the Law. The three-volume work on Joshua, Judges and Ruth [the *Triteuch*] tells of the inheritance of the land and of the deeds of the judges and the genealogy of David. The Kings and Chronicles tell of the deeds of the kings, and Esdras tells of the release of the captives, the return of the people, and the building of the temple and the city. The prophets include prophecies concerning the advent of the Savior, calls for obedience concerning the commandments and for condemnation against their transgressors, as well as including prophecies for the gentiles. But the book of Psalms is like a garden which besides bearing fruit in it that is found elsewhere—which it sets to music—brings to light its own special fruit which it accompanies in song along with the words.

§3 – The Psalms Recapitulate Genesis, Exodus, and Numbers

It sings, for instance, of the Genesis events in Psalm 19: *The heavens declare the glory of God and the firmament proclaims the work of his hands*; and the 24th Psalm: *The earth is the Lord's and its fullness, its inhabitants and all who dwell in it; he laid its foundation upon the sea.* The accounts in Exodus, Numbers and Deuteronomy are sung beautifully in Psalm 78 and in the 114th [and 115th] Psalm: *In the exodus of Israel from Egypt, of the house of Jacob that came from a barbarous people, Judah became his sanctuary, Israel his dominion.* And again Psalm 105 says: *He sent his servant Moses, and Aaron whom he had chosen: he placed in them the words of his signs and of his wonders in the Land of Cham.*[3] *He sent darkness, and it darkened, and they rebelled against his words. He changed their waters into blood and killed their fish. Their land issued forth frogs in the palaces of their kings,* it says, *and the dog-fly and lice went into all their borders.* And we find the whole entirety of this psalm and Psalm 106 are written about these things. The matters concerning the priesthood and the tabernacle are referenced in Psalm 29,[4] which was sung when the tabernacle was brought out: *Bring to the Lord, sons of God, bring to the Lord the ram's offspring. Bring to the Lord glory and honor.*

§4 – The Psalms Recapitulate Joshua and Judges

The events of Joshua, son of Nun, and Judges are shown in Psalm 107: *And they built cities to inhabit, and sowed fields, and planted vineyards.* For under Joshua, son of Nun, the promised land was handed over to them. And when we read in this same psalm frequently: *And they cried to the Lord in their afflictions, and from their distress he delivered them*, this indicates the events in the book of Judges. For when they cried out, he raised up judges at the time and saved the people from their afflictions. He sings the same

---

3   I.e., Ham.

4   The heading of Psalm 28 in the Septuagint is "A psalm of David when the tabernacle went forth."

things about the deeds of the kings in Psalm 20 saying: *Some trust in chariots and some in horses, but we will glory in the name of the Lord our God. They are brought down and fall. But we are raised up and restored. Lord, save the king and listen to us in whatever day we call upon you.* The events of Esdras are chanted in Psalm 126 of the Psalms of Ascent:[5] *When the Lord returned the captives of Zion we became as those who are comforted.* And again in Psalm 122: *I rejoiced when they said to me, "Let us go into the house of the Lord." Our feet stood in your courts, O Jerusalem. Jerusalem built as a city meant for joint possession. For that is where the tribes went up, the tribes of the Lord, as a testimony to Israel.*

§5 – The Psalms Recapitulate the Prophets

The matters about which the Prophets speak are included in almost every one of the Psalms. In the 50th Psalm it talks about the Savior's time here on earth and that he would live here while being God: *The Lord will clearly come, our God, and he will not remain silent.* And in the 118th Psalm: *Blessed is the one who comes in the name of the Lord. We have blessed you from the house of the Lord. The Lord is God, and he has illumined us.* And the 107th Psalm sings that this one [just mentioned] is the Word of the Father: *He sent his Word, and he healed them, and he delivered them from their ruin.* For the one who comes is God himself and the Word who is sent. And the voice of the Father sings in the 45th Psalm that this very Word is known to be the Son of God: *My heart has uttered a good Word.* And again, in the 110th Psalm: *From the womb, before the morning star, I have begotten you.* For what else would you call someone born of the Father than his Word and Wisdom? This same book

---

5   Psalms of Ascent – Psalms 120–134 (119–133 in the Septuagint) are a group of fifteen psalms known as the Psalms of Ascent, or the Gradual Psalms.

comprehends that it was known to whom the Father said, *Let there be light, and the firmament and all things* (Gen 1:3ff), when it says, *By the Word of the Lord the heavens were established, and all their powers by the breath of his mouth* (Ps 33:6).

§6 – The Psalms Point Forward to Christ

Nor was it ignorant of Christ and his coming, but even makes a special mention of him in the 45th Psalm: *Your throne, O God is forever and ever. The scepter of your kingdom is a scepter of righteousness. You have loved righteousness and hated injustice. Because of this, God, your God has anointed you with the oil of gladness beyond your companions.* And just in case someone might think his coming was only in appearance,[6] it indicates that he would become man, and that this is the one through whom all things came to be, saying in the 87th Psalm: *The Mother of Zion will say, "A man, and a man is born in her," and the Most High himself established her.* For this is the same as saying: *And the Word was God. All things came into being through him. . . . And the Word became flesh* (John 1:1–2, 14). Because the Psalter knew all of this, as well as that he was from a virgin, it could not keep silent but immediately gives a clear indication of this in the 45th: *Listen, daughter, and see, and bend your ear, and forget your people and the house of your father, because the king has set his heart upon your beauty.* This again is like what is said by Gabriel: *Greetings, favored one, the Lord is with you* (Luke 1:28). For after proclaiming him the Christ, he immediately made known the human birth from the virgin, saying: *Listen, daughter.* Notice that Gabriel calls Mary by name since he has a different origin

---

6 Athanasius speaks here against the ancient heresies of Docetism and Gnosticism.*

than she has. But David, from whose seed she happened to be, suitably addresses her as daughter.

§7 – The Psalms Foretell Christ's Atoning Death on the Cross

After proclaiming that he would become man, it follows that the Psalter would make known his suffering in the flesh as well. Perceiving, then, there would be a treacherous scheme carried out by the Jews, it sings [about this] in the 2nd Psalm: *Why do the nations rage, and the peoples plot a vain thing? The kings of the earth rise up, and the rulers gather themselves together against the Lord and against his Christ.* In the 22nd Psalm it speaks from the Savior's own person of the kind of death he would undergo: *You have brought me down into the dust of death. For many dogs have surrounded me, the assembly of the evildoers has encompassed me. They pierced my hands and my feet. They counted out all my bones. And after they considered and beheld me, they divided my clothing among themselves and cast lots for my clothing.* To gouge the hands and the feet, what else can this indicate than that it is speaking about the cross? After teaching all these things it then adds that the Lord suffered these things not for himself, but for us. And he says this again in his own person in Psalm 88: *Your wrath has rested upon me*; and in Psalm 69: *Then I restored that which I did not take away.* For although he was not guilty, he died. But he suffered for us and endured the wrath that was meant for us because of our disobedience, as is spoken through the prophet Isaiah: *He took on our weaknesses* (Isa 53:4). And this is mentioned for us in the 138th Psalm: *The Lord will pay them back for me.* And speaking also by the Spirit in Psalm 72: *And he will save the children of the poor, and he will humble the extortionists . . . for he has delivered the poor* from the hand of the oppressor, and the laborer for whom no help was offered.

§8 – The Psalms Foretell Christ's Ascension and Return

This is why it predicts his bodily ascension to the heavens and says in Psalm 24: *Lift up your gates, princes, and be lifted up you everlasting doors, and the king of glory will come in.* And in Psalm 47: *God ascends with a shout, the Lord with the voice of the trumpet.* It announces his being seated at the right hand and says in Psalm 110: *The Lord said to my Lord, "Sit at my right hand until I make your enemies a footstool for your feet."* And in the 9th Psalm it cries aloud about the destruction of the devil that occurred: *You sat upon the throne as one who judges righteousness; you censured the nations and the ungodly one perished.* For the fact that he has received judgment over all from the Father is not hidden [in the Psalms] either. Psalm 72 foretells that he would come as judge over all: *O God, give your judgment to the king and your righteousness to the son of the king to judge your people in righteousness and your poor with discernment.* And in the 50th Psalm it says: *He will summon the heaven above and the earth to sort out his people. And the heavens will announce his righteousness; for God is judge.* And in the 82nd Psalm we read: *God stands in the assembly of the gods, and in their midst he will judge the gods.* Even more, we learn from the Psalter about the calling of the nations in many places, but especially from Psalm 47: *Clap your hands all you nations, shout for joy to God with a voice of exultation.* And in the 72nd Psalm: *The Ethiopians will fall before him and his enemies will lick up the dust. The kings of Tarshish and the islands will offer gifts; the kings of Arabia and Saba will bring gifts. And all the kings of the earth will worship him, all the nations will serve him.* All these things are sung about in the Psalms, and in each of the other books of Scripture they are foretold as well.

§9 – Similarities between the Psalms and the Rest of Scripture

Moreover, the old man said, I am not unaware that in every book of Scripture the same things concerning the Savior are given special prominence. In fact, this common argument is in all of them as all share in the same symphony of the Spirit. For just as one can find some things in the book of Psalms that are also in the others, so also material in the book of Psalms is often found in the others. Moses, for example, writes a song and Isaiah sings and Habakkuk prays with a song. And again, in each of the books you can perceive prophecies, legislation and historical accounts. For the same Spirit is over all, and each book ministers and fulfills the grace that is given to it according to the apportionment of the Spirit in each, whether it is prophecy, legislation, or a narration of the historical accounts, or the grace of the Psalms. And inasmuch as it is one and the same Spirit, certainly they are not all divided since the Spirit is indivisible by nature. Because the Spirit is given in its entirety, the manifestations and divisions of the Spirit are also distributed to each in order to serve the needs they are addressing. Furthermore, each [book] often ministers the Word as the Spirit instructs according to the need that has been laid bare. Therefore, as I said previously, when Moses enacts laws sometimes he prophesies, other times he sings. When the prophets prophesy sometimes they command: *Wash yourselves, be clean* (Isa 1:16). *Cleanse your hearts from evil, Jerusalem* (Jer 4:14); and other times they narrate history, such as Daniel does about Susannah (Dan 12), and Isaiah about Rabshakeh and Sennacherib (Isa 36–37).

In the same way, the book of Psalms whose fundamental characteristic is that of song, sings within the full range of the voice accompanied by melodies about the matters recorded in detail in the other books, as I mentioned previously. But sometimes it also legislates: *Cease from evil and leave wrath behind* (Ps 37:8). And: *Decline from evil and do good. Seek peace and pursue it* (Ps 34:14). And sometimes it also narrates about Israel's journey, or it prophecies about the Savior, just as was said previously.

§10 – The Psalms Uniquely Engage the Emotions of the Soul

Therefore, let there be a common grace of the Spirit with all of Scripture and let the same grace which is in all of the books be found present in each book as the situation demands and as the Spirit wills. For the greater and the lesser in this do not differ according to need, since each unyieldingly fulfills and completes its own service. Indeed, the book of Psalms also has a certain grace of its own and an elevated style. For in addition to the other things it has in common with the other books, it has this amazing aspect—that within it the movements of each soul with all its changes and chastisements are detailed and worked out. The result is that anyone who really wants to receive or to understand from its limitless possibilities finds himself formed in just the way we find written there in the Psalms. For in the other books you only hear the law pronounced—what you need to do and not to do. And you listen and pay attention to the prophets as the only way to know the coming of the Savior, or you turn to the historical books in order to know about what the kings and the saints did. But when you listen to the book of the Psalms you not only learn about these things, but also apprehend and are taught the movements of your own souls. Consequently, when the passions take their toll on you, you are able to bring to bear the image of the words gleaned from the Psalms so they not only teach you, when you listen to them, to elude passions, but also what you need to say or do in order to heal the passions. Now there are words of warning also in the other books when they, for example, forbid evil. But in the Psalms you are also told how to keep away from evil. For instance, the command to repent is like this—repentance means to stop sinning. But the book of Psalms also tells how to repent and what is necessary to say for repentance to actually take place. Moreover, Paul says: *Tribulation produces endurance for the soul, endurance produces character, and character hope, and this hope does not disappoint* (Rom 5:3–5). In the Psalms too you are told how it is necessary to bear afflictions, and what you should say to someone who is suffering and what to say after the suffering has occurred. It relates how each person is tested and what words have been written and inscribed for those who hope in the Lord. In addition there is the command to give thanks in all things (1 Thess 5:18), but the Psalms also teach what you should actually say when giving thanks. Then, hearing from another [book]: *As many as desire to pursue a godly life, they will be persecuted* (2 Tim 3:12), from the Psalms we are also taught what to cry out when fleeing and what words should be offered to God while we are being persecuted, as well as what to say after the persecution when we have been delivered. We are encouraged to bless the Lord as well as to confess our praise to him. But in the Psalms we are even informed how one ought to praise the Lord and what words to say in order to confess him rightly. In fact, in every case we will find that these divine songs have been provided for us and the inner motions of our souls, and whatever condition we find ourselves in.

§11 – The Psalms Become Our Own Words in Prayer

There is also this incredible thing in the Psalms. When people read what the saints say in the other books of Scripture or what is written about them, they don't see themselves in what is being spoken or written about. And when they hear what is being said they don't think it refers to themselves either, although they may go so far as to imitate the deeds, they hear proclaimed and may even stand in awe of the zeal of these holy men: but no further. And when they take up the Psalter and encounter the prophecies about the Savior in certain Psalms, they treat them, too, with the same awe and reverence as they did when they encountered them in the other Scriptures. But the truly amazing thing is that when they come to the other Psalms, they recognize them as being their very own words. And when they hear they are actually moved in their conscience. They feel is as though they are the ones speaking and they take to heart the words of the songs as if they were their own. But for the sake of clarity, let us not hesitate to repeat what we've been saying, following the example of the blessed apostle.[7] Many of the words of the patriarchs were spoken as their own. When Moses would speak, God would answer. And when both Elijah and Elisha called to the Lord while they were on Mount Carmel they would usually say: *As the Lord lives, before whom I stand this day* (1 Kgs 17:1; 2 Kgs 3:14). The principle words of the other holy prophets are words about the Savior, although most are directed toward the nations

---

7   In his Epistles, Paul at times will repeat words or phrases for clarity, such as he does in Galatians 1:9 and Philippians 4:4.

and Israel. Nevertheless no one would ever claim the patriarchs' words as his own when he spoke, nor would anyone be bold enough to represent himself as speaking the words of Moses as if they were his own, nor would he have the effrontery to speak as his own the words of Abraham about the great Isaac or of Ishmael concerning the house-born slave—even if he felt there was some need or necessity that might compel him to do so. And if anyone would sympathize with someone who is suffering, and then at some point have a desire to say something more, he would never speak as Moses did: *Show yourself to me!* (Exod 33:13). Or again: *If you will forgive their sin, forgive. But if you will not forgive, then remove me from your book of life which you have written* (Exod 32:32). Nor would anyone claim as his own the words of the prophets when they offered blame or praise, as though such a person could blame someone or offer praise like the prophets did. No one would represent himself as if he were speaking as his own the words: *As the Lord lives, before whom I stand this day.* For it surely is clear by now that anyone who encounters these books would not claim their words as his own, but would make clear that these are the words of the saints who are speaking. But with the Psalms, the amazing thing is that, apart from those that deal with the prophecies about the Savior and the nations, whenever anyone recites the rest of the Psalms he speaks the words as though they were his own and as though each of the Psalms was written specifically for him, and not as though someone else were speaking or as though they were meant for another. Instead, he recites them as one who is speaking these things about himself as if he were accomplishing these very things himself. And in the very act of speaking them he is offering them to God on his own behalf. For he will not exhibit the same caution about these as he would with the words of the patriarchs, or Moses, or the other prophets. But above all, the one who sings them has the confidence that what he is speaking is as if it were his own and was written for him. For the Psalms address the deeds of those who keep the commandments as well as those who transgress them. And it is necessary that everyone be governed by these commandments, and whether they keep the commandment or transgress it, they should speak the words written that pertain to their particular situation.

§12 – The Psalms Reveal and Guide the Inner Self

It seems to me that these words often act like a mirror for the one who sings them. They allow him to see himself and the inner movements of his own soul in them. And when one recites them, they produce that very effect. Indeed, for when someone hears what is read, he receives the song as if it were speaking directly about him. He either repents, convicted by his conscience which is sorely pricked, or after hearing about the hope in God and the help that awaits those who believe, he rejoices and begins to give thanks to God that such a gift is available to him. So then, when someone sings the 3rd Psalm, recognizing his own afflictions, he will treat the words of the psalm as his own as well. And when someone sings the 12th and the 17th Psalm, the boldness and prayer they proclaim speak to his own situation. And when one sings Psalm 51 he recites the words of repentance they contain as if they were his own. And when singing Psalms 54, 56, 57 and 142, he sings not as if another were being persecuted, but considers himself as the one who is suffering, and he sings to the Lord as if these words were his own. And finally, since each psalm was dictated and composed by the Spirit, we find in them,

Appendix 2: On the Psalms

as was said above, a better understanding of the inner movements of our own soul. All of what they say concerns us, and so their words come across as though they were our words. They serve as a reminder of the inner movements within us and as a corrective for our daily conduct.[8] For these are the things the singers are communicating and they can serve as examples and patterns for us.

§13 – The Virtue of Christ Resounds in the Psalms

Moreover, the same grace comes from the Savior, for he became man for us and offered his own body into death for us in order that everyone might be delivered from death. And wanting to bring to light his own citizenship that is heavenly and well pleasing, he typified it in himself so that some might no longer be so easily deceived by the enemy, having his victory over the devil which he accomplished for us as their security against stumbling. For this reason, he not only taught but also practiced what he taught, so that as each person hears what the Savior says, he might receive from him—just as if he were looking at an image in a mirror—the paradigm of what to do, hearing: *Learn from me, for I am meek and humble in heart* (Matt 11:29). You could not find a more perfect example in virtuous teaching than what the Lord exemplified in himself. For whether in patient endurance, or love of humankind, or goodness, or manliness, or mercifulness, or righteousness—all of these you find occurring in him, with the result that there should be no aspect in virtue that is missing in anyone who comprehends this human life of his. For Paul knows this when he says: *Be imitators of me, just as I am of Christ* (1 Cor 11:1). Those Greek legislators exhibited an extraordinary

---

8   The Greek word has the idea of citizenship attached to it.

gift for speaking. But the Lord, who is truly Lord over all and concerned for those in distress, not only gave the law but also offered himself as a type, so that they might know the plans he is accomplishing by his power. It was surely because of this that, before the time he spent among us, he made this known in the Psalms in order that just as he made known in himself the earthly and the heavenly man by types, so also from the Psalms the one who is willing is able to learn the inner movements and dispositions of souls, finding in the Psalms both the healing and the correction needed for each movement.

§14 – There Are Various Types of Psalms

If it is necessary to speak even more to the point, let us first of all admit that the entire divine Scripture teaches virtue and the truths of the faith, but that the book of Psalms contains the primary pattern for how souls are to be managed. For just as one who comes before a king carries with him a certain comportment and demeanor in what he says, so that he might not be thrown out as uneducated when he talks, in the same way for those striving toward virtue and wanting to comprehend the life of the Savior in the body, when they read this divine book it first of all brings to mind the inner movements of the soul and in this way further models and teaches petitioners such words as they should use. For it must first be observed that in this book there are Psalms that speak in narrative form, in exhortations, in prophecies, in the form of prayer, as well as in confession:

- There are those in narrative form, such as Psalms 19, 44, 49, 50, 73, 77, 78, 89, 90, 107, 114 [and 115], 127, 137;

Appendix 2: On the Psalms

- There are those in the form of prayer such as Psalms 17, 68, 90, 102, 132, 142;

- There are those that combine petition, prayer and entreaty, such as Psalms 5, 6, 7, 12, 13, 16, 25, 28, 31, 35, 38, 43, 54, 55, 56, 57, 59, 60, 61, 64, 83, 86, 88, 138, 140, 143;

- And having petition with thanksgiving, such as Psalm 139;

- And then there are those that are only in the form of petition, such as Psalms 3, 26, 69, 70, 71, 74, 79, 80, 109, 123, 130, 131;

- Those in the form of confession are Psalms 9 [and 10], 75, 92, 105, 106, 107, 108, 111, 118, 136, 138;

- Those having a combination of confession and narrative are Psalms 9 [and 10], 75, 106, 107, 118, 138;

- Psalm 111 has a combination of confession and narrative with adoration;

- And Psalm 37 is in the form of exhortation;

- Those that have prophecy are Psalms 21, 22, 45, 47, 76;

- And Psalm 110 has a reporting of events joined with prophecy;

- And exhortation as well as prescriptions are found in Psalms 29, 33, 81, 95, 96, 97, 98, 103, 104, 114;

- Exhortation with song is found in Psalm 150;

- And those describing the virtuous life are Psalms 105, 112, 119, 125, 133;

- Those proclaiming praise are Psalms 91, 113, 117, 135, 145, 146, 147, 148, 150;

- Those giving thanks are Psalms 8, 9 [and 10], 18, 34, 46, 63, 77, 85, 116,[9] 121, 122, 124, 126, 129, 144;

- Those proclaiming blessedness are Psalms 1, 32, 41, 119, 128;

- And Psalm 108 demonstrates how to sing with zeal;

- While Psalm 81 exhorts to fortitude;

- Psalms 2, 14, 36, 52, 53 accuse the ungodly and lawbreakers;

- While Psalm 4 is one of invocation;

- Those describing devotion are such as Psalms 20 and 64;

- Those boasting in the Lord proclaim words such as those found in Psalms 23, 27, 39, 40, 42, 62, 76, 84, 97, 99, 151 (LXX);

- Those that rebuke are Psalms 58 and 82;

- And those that contain the words of a hymn are Psalms 48 and 65;

- Psalm 66 is a psalm of jubilation and about the resurrection;

---

9 The Hebrew and English Bibles combine Psalms 114 and 115 from the Septuagint.

- And another that contains only words of jubilation is Psalm 100.

§15 – A Psalm for Every Circumstance

Therefore, since the Psalms are arranged like this, it is possible for the readers to find in each, as was said above, the inner movements and conditions appropriate to the state of their own soul and identify the type of psalm as well as the teaching contained in each. Some Psalms tell how a person is able to please the Lord and make amends for his deeds and words, or how to give thanks to the Lord, or ensure that one does not fall into ungodliness for what he might say. For we will have to render an account to the Judge not only because of our works but also because of idle speech (Matt 12:36). If therefore any of you should decide to bless someone, you have what you need to say, and how and in whom you are to say it in Psalms 1, 32, 41, 119 and 128. If you want to rebuke the plotting of the Jews against the Savior you have the 2nd Psalm. If you are suffering persecution from your own people, and you have many assembled against you, recite the 3rd Psalm. If in such affliction you called to the Lord and you want to give thanks that he heard you, sing Psalms 4, 75 and 116. And when you notice the wicked lying in wait wanting to do you harm and you want the Lord to listen to your prayer, rise up early in the morning and sing Psalm 5. And when you perceive threats from the Lord, if you see yourself disturbed because of these, you can recite Psalms 6 and 38. And if someone is plotting something against you, as Ahithophel did against David (2 Sam 15:31), and you are informed about this, sing Psalm 7 and entrust yourself to God your deliverer.

Table 1: A Psalm for Every Circumstance[10]

If...	Then Read...
Blessing someone	Psalms 1, 32, 41, 119, 128
Rebuking those who crucified Christ	Psalm 2
Suffering persecution from your own people	Psalm 3
Giving thanks that God heard your prayer	Psalms 4, 75, 116
Under attack from enemies	Psalm 5
Disturbed by threats	Psalms 6, 38
Enemies plot against you	Psalm 7
Seeing the Savior's grace everywhere	Psalm 8
Celebrating the Savior's grace	Psalms 8, 84
Overcoming the enemy	Psalms 9, 10
Trouble is stirred up against you	Psalm 11
Evil is increasing	Psalm 12
Trapped by the sins of your enemies	Psalm 13
Hearing someone blaspheme the LORD	Psalms 14, 53
Learning of citizenship in heaven	Psalm 15
Needing prayer	Psalms 17, 86, 88, 141
Wanting to learn how Moses prayed	Psalm 90
Being saved from your enemies	Psalm 18
Amazed by creation	Psalms 19, 24
Consoling others	Psalm 20
Shepherded by the LORD	Psalm 23
Surrounded by enemies	Psalm 25
Enemies persist with unjust judgement	Psalms 26, 35, 43
Enemies make war	Psalm 27
Schemers acts shamelessly	Psalm 28

---

10 This table summarizes Athanasius's *Letter to Marcellinus on the Interpretation of the Psalms*, §§15–26.

Appendix 2: On the Psalms

If...	Then Read...
Making an offering to God	Psalm 29
Dedicating your home	Psalms 30, 127
Persecuted by family	Psalm 31
Witnessing a baptism	Psalm 32
Singing with others	Psalm 33
Avoiding an evil plot	Psalm 34
Observing transgressors with an evil spirit	Psalm 36
Persuading one to not pursue evil	Psalm 37
An enemy acts unjustly	Psalm 39
Learning endurance	Psalm 40
Wanting to be merciful to the poor	Psalm 41
Hearing of the enemies reproach	Psalm 42
Wanting to be reminded of God's kindness	Psalms 44, 78, 89, 105, 106, 107, 114, 115
Fleeing to God for deliverance	Psalm 46
Confessing and repenting of sin	Psalm 51
An evil king slanders	Psalm 52
Slandered against and betrayed	Psalms 54, 56
An enemy enters your life	Psalms 57, 142
Escaping from your enemy	Psalm 59
Made a fool	Psalm 55
Responding to hypocrites	Psalm 58
Enemies try to take your life	Psalm 62
Persecuted and forced to flee	Psalm 63
Being searched for by your enemies	Psalms 64, 65, 70, 71
Praising God with song	Psalm 65
Teaching about the resurrection	Psalm 66

If ...	Then Read ...
Asking God for mercy	Psalm 67
Unsettled by the ungodly prospering	Psalm 73
Comforting people	Psalm 74
Confessing sin	Psalms 9, 10, 75, 92, 105, 106, 107, 108, 111, 118, 136, 138
Putting the opinions of the heretics to shame	Psalm 76
Praying in great distress	Psalm 77
Enemies profane the house of God	Psalm 79
Singing to God	Psalms 81, 95
Enemies threaten the house of God	Psalm 83
Longing for the eternal house of God	Psalm 84
God's wrath subsides	Psalms 85, 126
Confronting division	Psalm 86
Encouraging godliness	Psalm 91
Singing on the Sabbath	Psalm 92
Giving thanks on the Lord's Day	Psalm 24
Singing praises on the 2nd day of the week	Psalm 48
Offering glory to God	Psalm 93
Singing for the victory of the cross	Psalm 93
Being held captive	Psalm 96
The land has rest from war	Psalm 97
Singing praises	Psalm 94
Teaching people obedience	Psalm 100
Learning of God's power in judging	Psalm 101
Feeling anxious	Psalm 102

Appendix 2: On the Psalms

If...	Then Read...
Praising God in all circumstances	Psalms 103, 104
Learning how to praise God	Psalms 105, 107, 135, 146, 147, 148, 150
Believing what you are praying	Psalm 116
Feeling as if ascending toward God	Psalms of Ascent* (120–134)
Lamenting over your former self	Psalm 137
Thankful for enduring trials	Psalm 139
Troubled by enemies	Psalm 140
Offering supplication	Psalms 5, 143
An enemy rises up against you	Psalm 144
Amazed at all God has done for you	Psalm 145
Singing to the Lord	Psalms 93, 98
Singing praises with Alleluias	Psalms 105, 106, 107, 111, 112, 113, 114, 115, 116, 117, 118, 119, 136, 146, 147, 148, 149, 150
Singing of the Savior in private	Psalms 45, 110
Wanting to hear a foretelling of the cross	Psalms 22, 69
Wanting to hear of the betrayal of Jesus	Psalms 2, 109
Wanting to hear of Christ's power in judging	Psalms 21, 50, 72
Wanting to hear of the resurrection	Psalm 16
Wanting to hear of Christ's ascension	Psalms 24, 47
Wanting to contemplate Christ's blessings	Psalms 93, 96, 98, 99

Discussion Questions

What is one difficult circumstance you are going through right now? Can you or the group think of a psalm that would be helpful for that particular circumstance?

Athanasius says the Psalms ultimately point to Christ. Read Psalm 2. How is this psalm fulfilled in Christ. After discussing, read Acts 4:23–32 to see how the New Testament authors interpreted Psalm 2.

Athanasius says the Psalms engage "the emotions of the soul" (§10). How have your emotions played a role in your faith?

Read Psalm 1. What role does God's word play in the life of God's people?

What ways have you heard of Christians regularly incorporating the Psalms in their daily lives? For example, some Christians read one psalm each day. How could you incorporate the Psalms into your daily routines?[1]

---

1 For more on rhythms of praying the Psalms, see Hank Voss, "Soul Work and Soul Care: Doing 'Psalm Work' with Augustine and Friends" in Carmen Joy Imes, ed., *Praying the Psalms with Augustine and Friends*, Sacred Roots Spiritual Classics 1 (Upland, IN: Samuel Morris Publications, 2021), 277–92.

Afterword

THEOLOGY & ETHICS

Afterword

Athanasius offers a beautiful vision of the Christian life. While we were made for immortality (eternal life) with God, our sin separated us from God, bringing corruption and death. But God, in his grace, sent his Son to rescue sinners and renew creation. *On the Incarnation* is a brief yet profound portrayal of the person and work of Christ. *The Life of Antony* shows us what renewal looks like practically in the life of one person. And *On the Psalms* teaches us that all of this (what we know about Christ and how we live in Christ) is grounded in Scripture. There are at least three lessons that I hope each reader takes away from these works.

Christ is central. Athanasius offers a radically Christ-centered view of theology and of the world. Jesus is the revelation of the Father and the one anointed by the Spirit. He is the apex of the biblical story and the turning point of our stories. This means that the Christian life is not ultimately about us: it is about Jesus. He is the beginning, middle, and end of a healthy and growing life.

Christ is making all things new. For the "Champion of Nicaea," it is too small a task for God to merely save our souls. Rather, the Creator of all things has responded to human sin with a plan to re-create all things. Through the life, death, and resurrection of Jesus, God is taking what is broken and restoring it by grace. We are a part of a grand re-creation project, and we will not only be ushered into the presence of God, but we will also delight in the goodness of God as renewed people in his renewed creation.

Christ is making us new. Athanasius gives a vision of the Christian life that is about renewal in Christ. Through his death for our sins and his resurrection from the grave, our guilt is forgiven, our shame is removed, and we are set free in order to share in the incorruptible life of our reigning King. The Christian life, therefore, is one of renewal. We are given a new heart (Ezek 36:26), new spirit (Ezek 11:19), new mind (Rom 12:2), new identity (Col 3:10), new family (Mark 3:31–35), and the hope of living in a new world (Matt 19:28). But while Christ is the one who makes us new, we receive his gracious work by faith. And having faith means that we see things from God's perspective, no matter how it may look to the world. As Paul says, "Though our outer self is wasting away, our inner self is being renewed day by day" (2 Cor 4:16).

Resources for Application

THEOLOGY & ETHICS

Soul Work and Soul Care: Experiencing Renewal in Christ through a Simple and Disciplined Life

Jeremy Treat

Each Sacred Roots Spiritual Classic has a "Soul Work and Soul Care" resource to illustrate how Christian leaders across cultures and generations have found a particular spiritual classic helpful in pastoral ministry. "Soul work" includes the *personal* work of watering, weeding, pruning, and fertilizing the garden of one's own soul. In a similar way, "soul care" involves the *pastoral* work of nurturing growth in another's friendship with God. When Jesus discusses "soul work" and "soul care," he often uses metaphors from the medical and agricultural professions. Like a doctor for souls, or a farmer caring for an orchard of fruit trees, congregational leaders who hope to tend souls can learn much from the wisdom of those who have gone before us.

How does this vision for renewal in Christ play out in practice? Athanasius and Antony would speak of the ascetic life. The word "ascetic" comes from the Greek *askeō* which means to train or exercise. For Athanasius, the ascetic life is a life of simplicity and discipline, a training of the heart to daily experience renewal in Christ. And while Antony models an extreme version of the ascetic life by spending much of his life alone in the desert, Athanasius lived an ascetic life in both the desert (while in exile) and in the bustling city of Alexandria. An ascetic life is not so much about what is happening around you, but what is happening inside of you.

How can you experience renewal in Christ through a simple and disciplined life? There are three spiritual practices we can apply from Athanasius's vision of the Christian life.

Living in Light of the Gospel

A simple and disciplined life comes from fixing our eyes on Jesus, the author and perfecter of our faith (Heb 12:2). Understanding who Jesus is and what he has done for us, as Athanasius helps us do in *On the Incarnation*, does not merely apply to conversion. The good news is for all of life. The way we grow as Christians is not by trying harder but rather by trusting in God's grace and applying the gospel to every aspect of life. This is why Paul, toward the end of his first letter to the Corinthians, responds to their struggles with sexual immorality, alcohol abuse, and division by reminding them of the gospel (1 Cor 15:1–4). He tells them that the gospel is not only something we receive when we become Christians; it is the foundation we stand on as we grow as Christians (1 Cor 15:2).

But it gets even better. The grace of the gospel that we receive from God does not come to us like spiritual fairy dust, somehow separate from God himself. It is received *in Christ*. Let us consider the implications. Renewal is not merely something Christ gives us, as if the blessings would be sufficient without the source. No, we experience not merely renewal *from* Christ, or even renewal *like* Christ. We experience renewal *in* Christ, which means our greatest good is not the gifts but the Giver himself.

A daily practice, therefore, is to remind yourself of the gospel and your identity in Christ that flows from it. When you feel guilty, do not simply try harder. Remember Christ and remind yourself, "I am forgiven." When you are tempted by the enemy to sin, remind yourself, "I have been set free from sin and the enemy has no power over me." When you feel alone, remember the truths of the gospel that God is with you and you have been adopted into a spiritual family. In Christ, you are a new creation.

Again, the key to a simple and disciplined life is to fix your eyes on Jesus. Reflect on these lines from a classic hymn:

> Turn your eyes upon Jesus
> Look full in his wonderful face
> And the things of earth will grow strangely dim
> In the light of his glorious grace.

Reading Scripture and Praying the Psalms

Jesus says, "Man shall not live by bread alone, but by every word that comes from the mouth of God" (Matt 4:4). In other words, our souls need Scripture as much as our bodies need food. Through Scripture, God has revealed himself and invited us into conversation with him. He initiated. He broke the silence. And reading God's word, meditating on God's word, and memorizing God's word trains us for righteousness (2 Tim 3:16). There are two spiritual practices I recommend for daily experiencing renewal in Christ through the Scriptures.

First, learn the story of Scripture so that you can live by the story of Scripture. People often know many of the individual stories of the Bible (e.g., Noah's ark, David and Goliath, Jesus walking on water). But Athanasius teaches us that Scripture is one grand story that culminates in Christ. We need to know the overarching narrative of Scripture to know who Jesus is and to know who we are. See if you can summarize the storyline of the Bible in two minutes. Perhaps try it out with a friend. Although there are many ways to tell the story of Scripture, one helpful way is to think of the Bible has having four chapters.

- Creation
- Fall
- Redemption
- New Creation

A second spiritual practice is to daily read the Psalms. The Psalms are the prayerbook of the Bible. And as Athanasius teaches us, there is a psalm for every circumstance. The Psalms teach us that every emotion and every situation is an opportunity to connect with God. And when we do not know what to pray, the Psalms teach us how to pray. They give language for the soul, whether lament, praise, requests, or hope. There are a variety of ways to build a regular practice of praying the psalms. I recommend one practice that has been transformative in my life. I read the same psalm every day for one week (along with the other Scripture I am reading). What makes this a powerful experience for me is that each day I read and meditate on the psalm, it sinks deeper into my soul. My heart shifts from a posture of learning from the psalm early in the week to reflecting on and praying the psalm later in the week. As we daily reflect on God's word, we too will be able to say, "Your word is a lamp to my feet and a light to my path" (Ps 119:105).

Prayer and Fasting

When faced with spiritual warfare or temptation, Athanasius teaches us (through the example of Antony) to fast and pray. But, of course, these practices ultimately come not from Athanasius but from Jesus himself. Jesus does not say "*If* you fast"; he says "*When* you fast" (Matt 6:16). Fasting, therefore, needs to be a regular part of the Christian life, constantly reminding us to hunger more for Christ than the pleasures of this world. When fasting, we simply abstain from food (or something else) in order to focus on spiritual realities.

Jesus also did not say "*If* you pray," but rather "*When* you pray" (Matt 6:9). Prayer, therefore, also must be a consistent part of the Christian's life. At one level, prayer is simply talking to God. But at a deeper level, prayer is communion with God. We are not merely coming before our king to present requests. We are with our Father who wants to hear about whatever is going on in our lives and draw us nearer to his heart. There are many forms of prayer: praise, lament, confession, thanksgiving, interceding for others, and requests for ourselves. But each of these is not merely a way of getting something from God but of being with God.

Fasting and praying are linked together in Scripture because (1) practically, we can use the time normally reserved for a meal to pray instead, and (2) spiritually, fasting enhances our hunger and yearning, which we then redirect to God, who satisfies our souls.

There are a variety of ways to incorporate these two practices into your life. First, choose a time, whether weekly or monthly, to fast. Ideally, partner with others in fasting so you can support one another and share the experience together. Second, while we can "pray without ceasing" throughout the day (1 Thess 5:18), we should also set aside specific times to commune with our Father in prayer. The Lord's Prayer can be a template to help you pray in such a way that is in line with God's word and in praying a variety of types of prayers.

Together, fasting and prayer are a powerful combination for a life of discipline. In a world that teaches us to follow our desires, fasting and praying is one of God's ways of training us to say no to weaker desires in order to say yes to greater desires.

Working from Grace

As we talk about spiritual practices, we must remember again the importance of the centrality of Christ. Practices are not a way that we work for God's acceptance or train ourselves into spiritual shape. No. We do not work *for* grace. We work *from* grace. We look to Christ, remembering who he is and all he has done for us, and the Spirit conforms us into the image of Christ to the glory of God.

Continuing the Conversation
Jeremy Treat

Athanasius's Works

Athanasius. *Select Writings and Letters.* Translated by Archibald Robertson. Vol. 4 of *The Nicene and Post-Nicene Fathers*, Series 2. Edited by Philip Schaff and Henry Wace. 1886–1889. Repr. ed., Peabody, MA: Hendrickson, 2012.

This single volume has most of Athanasius's known works. It can be accessed for free online at https://ccel.org/ccel/schaff/npnf204/npnf204.

Athanasius. *The Life of Antony and the Letter to Marcellinus.* Edited by Robert C. Gregg. Classics of Western Spirituality. Mahwah, NJ: Paulist Press, 1980.

This has the full text of *The Life of Antony* and *Letter to Marcellinus on the Interpretation of the Psalms*.

Athanasius. *On the Incarnation.* Edited by John Behr. Greek and English Edition. Popular Patristics 44A. Yonkers, NY: St. Vladimir's Seminary Press, 2012.

This volume includes a recent English translation of *On the Incarnation* as well as the original Greek text. It also contains a helpful introduction to Athanasius.

Works about Athanasius

Anatolios, Khaled. *Athanasius.* Early Church Fathers. New York: Routledge, 2004.

Barnes, Peter. *Athanasius of Alexandria: His Life and Impact*. Fearn, Scotland: Christian Focus, 2019.

Gwynn, David M. *Athanasius of Alexandria: Bishop, Theologian, Ascetic, Father.* Christian Theology in Context. Oxford, UK: Oxford University Press, 2012.

Leithart, Peter. *Athanasius*. Foundations of Theological Exegesis and Christian Spirituality. Grand Rapids: Baker Academic, 2011.

Weinandy, Thomas. *Athanasius: A Theological Introduction*. Washington, DC: Catholic University of America Press, 2018.

Glossary

Aesculapius – According to Greek mythology, the son of Apollo who became the god of healing.

Arians – People who followed the teachings of Arius: namely, that Jesus had not eternally existed as God.

Arsenoitic Canal – A canal connecting the Nile River and the Faiyum Oasis.

Asbestos – A mineral known for being fire-resistant.

Ascesis – A spiritual discipline which early Christians practiced. The Greek word is based on the idea of athletic training which Christians appropriated for disciplining both body and soul.

Ascetic – A person with an intense focus on the discipline of soul and body. The Greek root of the word is also the basis for the word "monk."

Augustine of Hippo (AD 354–430) – The Bishop of Hippo who would go on to be one of the most influential theologians in all of history.

Epicureans – People who followed the teachings of the Greek philosopher Epicurus. They denied the existence of a creator and sought meaning and pleasure in the material world.

Gnostics – People who made a sharp distinction between the material and spiritual realms (prioritizing the spiritual realm) and believed that salvation came through secret knowledge.

Meletians – A group that broke away from the church of Alexandria over the issue of how to respond to lapsed Christians who desired to return to the church. The Meletians opposed Athanasius when he first became bishop of Alexandria.

Monastic Movement, The – The patristics-era phenomenon of many Christians radically devoting themselves to Christ through a simple life of prayer and discipline. Some of these monks sought this alone, while others formed communities around their common pursuit. See Greg Peters, *The Story of Monasticism: Retrieving an Ancient Tradition for Contemporary Spirituality* (Grand Rapids: Baker Academic, 2015).

Psalms of Ascent – Psalms 120–134 (119–133 in the Septuagint) are a group of fifteen psalms known as the Psalms of Ascent, or the Gradual Psalms.

Serapion of Thmuis (AD 300-360) – A disciple of Antony and companion of Athanasius. Athanasius wrote Serapion three letters about the Holy Spirit. See Athanasius, "Letters to Serapion on the Holy Spirit."

Thebans – People from the city of Thebes, the ancient capital of Upper Egypt.

Virgins – Single Christian women who decided to devote themselves fully to pursuing Christ.

Watching – The ancient practice that consists of an individual rising in the middle of the night to spend time in focused prayer. The tradition is rooted in Luke's account of Jesus praying during the night (Luke 6:12–13).

Resources for Application   191

Map of Important Places:
Athanasius of Alexandria

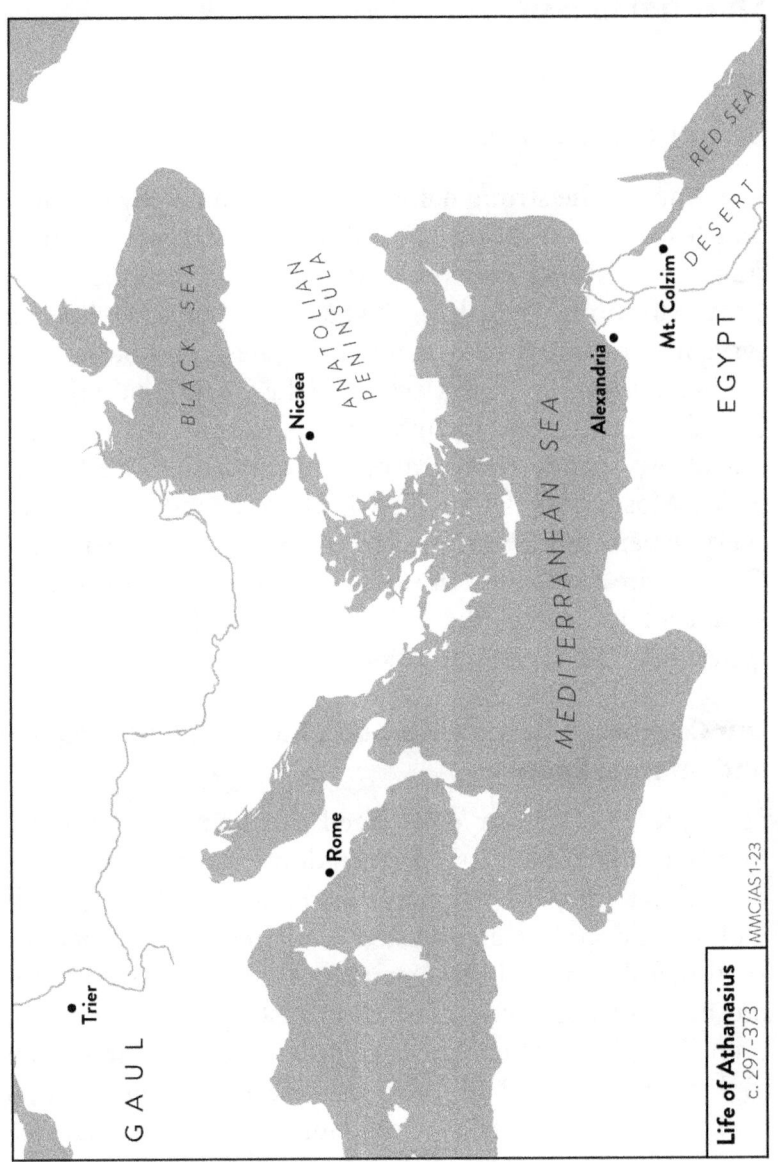

A Letter to God's Friends and Fellow Warriors On Why We Read the Sacred Roots Spiritual Classics Together

Dear Friends and Fellow Warriors,

Greetings in the strong name of Jesus! What a joy to know that Jesus calls us "Friend" (John 15). What an honor to stand with sisters and brothers from every century and culture to shout, "Worthy is the Lamb!" What a privilege to serve in the Lamb's army, not fighting flesh and blood, but God's *internal* (the flesh), *external* (the world) and *infernal* (the devil) enemies. In light of this cosmic struggle, we put on a wartime (not peacetime) mindset as we follow Jesus. Moses stated that God is present and at work in every generation (Ps 90:1), and the Sacred Roots Spiritual Classics are for those who desire to be used within their sphere of influence like David was used by God in his generation (Ps 57:2; Acts 13:36).

Our Context: A Battle with God's Internal, External, and Infernal Enemies

Scripture teaches our daily need to choose a missional mindset (Matt 6:10). God's kingdom never advances in neutral territory. Every inch in creation, including each inch of our soul, is a contested battlefield. God's enemies are threefold. First, there is an *internal* enemy hiding within the heart of each redeemed child of God. God loves us, even though we often battle a "Judas-heart"—a tendency to betray our Lord (John 12:6). Scripture names this brokenness the "flesh," the old "man" or the "sin nature"

(Rom 8; Gal 5–6). We work to kill ("mortify") this sin lest it succeed in killing us (Rom 6:13).

Second, as followers of Jesus, we battle all *external* enemies opposing the Lamb's kingdom. Sickened by sin, polluted by greed, corrupted by self-centeredness, idolatry and oppression; our world is not the way it is supposed to be. What God created good has been twisted and now often grieves the Holy Spirit. We choose to stand with Shadrach, Meshach and Abednego in refusing to bow to the principalities and powers of the age (Dan 3), or to accept the besetting sins of our ethnicities, nations and generations. Scripture and our sacred roots shine painful yet purifying light on our blind spots.

Finally, we are not ignorant of the devil's schemes. We may not know if a demon's name is "Screwtape" or "Legion," but we do know that an *infernal* enemy opposes God's kingdom *shalom*. He is the devil, Satan, the father of lies, the Accuser, and one day soon he and his demons will be completely crushed. In this time between the times, the Lamb's followers resist and renounce the devil and all his ways with the sword of the Spirit which is the word of God.

Our Mission: To Be Faithful Stewards and Wise Servants in Our Generation

Scripture contains a number of "history" psalms (Pss 78, 105, 106, 136; Neh 9:6–38; cf. Heb 11). These songs challenge us to reflect on women and men who chose to serve God in their generation—Abraham and Sarah, Moses, Phinehas, Rahab, David, Esther and many others. History psalms also warn of those who ignored or refused to participate in God's work (Pharaoh, Dathan, Abiram, Og).

Leaders like Rahab the prostitute (Matt 1:5; Heb 11:35; James 2:25) and King David were far from perfect (Ps 51). Yet Scripture declares that leaders like David "served the purposes of God in his own generation" (Acts 13:36).

Do you want God to use you in your generation? Are you willing to be a David or an Esther today? God is already at work in our communities, schools and workplaces. Sometimes the neighborhoods with the greatest challenges (those with giants like "Goliath" and armies of Philistine enemies) are the very places God finds servants and stewards he can use (1 Sam 17; 1 Cor 4:1).

Like King David, Prince Kaboo of the Kru people in Liberia chose to participate in God's work in his generation. As a child, Prince Kaboo (1873–1893) was taken hostage by a rival tribe and was about to be executed when he experienced a supernatural deliverance. After weeks of traveling through the jungle, Kaboo arrived at a mission station near Monrovia, Liberia's capital. There, as a fourteen-year-old teenager, he wholeheartedly gave his life to Jesus Christ.

Prince Kaboo took on the name Samuel Kaboo Morris at his baptism, and he spent the next four years working and studying Scripture—especially Jesus's teaching about the Holy Spirit as recorded by his friend John (John 14–17). Kaboo was fascinated with the Holy Spirit, for he had personally experienced the Holy Spirit's powerful deliverance. Eventually, the missionaries told Kaboo they had taught him all they knew and that if he wanted to learn more about the Holy Spirit, he would need to travel to the United States. Kaboo felt the need for more training about the Holy Spirit before being ready to return to the Kru as an evangelist. With no shoes or money, Kaboo walked to Monrovia's harbor to find passage to New York—trusting his Father in heaven to provide.

Kaboo's story is powerful. The ship that transported Kaboo experienced revival with the captain and many crew coming to Christ. Within a few hours of arriving in New York, Kaboo led seventeen men to Christ at an inner-city rescue mission. On his third day in the United States, the eighteen-year-old evangelist preached at a Sunday school meeting and revival broke out with a new missionary society organized that very day. God provided money for Kaboo's college tuition, housing, books and necessities. By the end of his first week in America, Kaboo had arrived in Fort Wayne, Indiana, to begin studying at Taylor University—an evangelical college committed to raising up workers for the harvest fields who walk in the power of the Holy Spirit (Matt 9:38; Acts 1:8).

Prince Kaboo's arrival at Taylor University transformed not only Taylor University's campus, but also the whole city of Fort Wayne. On his first Sunday in town, Kaboo walked to the front of the church and asked for permission to pray. As he prayed, the power and presence of the Holy Spirit descended on the congregation in a way none had ever experienced before. The pastor reported, "What I said and what Sammy said I do not remember, but I know my soul was on fire as never before. . . . No such visitation of the Holy Spirit had ever been witnessed" by our congregation.[1]

Two years later, on May 12, 1893, at the age of twenty, Prince Samuel Kaboo Morris died from an illness contracted after traveling through a snowstorm to preach. Since his death, Kaboo's story has influenced thousands of students at Taylor University and elsewhere to participate with the Holy Spirit in mission and seek the Spirit's power in witness. John Wengatz was a student at Taylor in 1906, the year he first read Kaboo's story. Some fifty years later, after a lifetime invested as a missionary in Africa, Wengatz remarked "my tears never cease to flow as I read that unrepeatable story."[2] Although Kaboo died at twenty, he was used mightily by God in his generation. Will those who tell the story of your life say the same?

Our Vision: Toward Ten Thousand "Tozers"

If you are pursuing God with the same passion and hunger displayed by Samuel Kaboo Morris, than you will be glad to meet A. W. Tozer (1897–1963). Tozer grew up poor without the opportunity to complete high school. While working in a tire factory he heard the good news about Jesus, repented and believed. At nineteen, he began to preach, becoming one of the most influential pastors in his generation. His books *The Pursuit of God* and *The*

---

1 Lindley Baldwin, *Samuel Morris: The African Boy God Sent to Prepare an American University for Its Mission to the World* (Minneapolis, MN: Bethany House, 1987), 59.

2 John Wengatz, *Sammy Morris: Spirit-Filled Life* (Upland, IN: Taylor University Press, 1954), Preface.

Knowledge of the Holy have helped millions know and love the Triune God revealed in Scripture. When asked how he learned to read Scripture with such clarity and theological depth, Pastor Tozer would often point to his "friends" and "teachers." These teachers were a list of some thirty-five Christian spiritual classics that he read and reread throughout his life. Sacred Roots Spiritual Classics (SRSC) are for those with a hunger for the Holy Spirit like Prince Kaboo and a desire to be used like Pastor Tozer.

Sacred Roots envisions ten thousand Christian leaders, serving in challenging ministry contexts across North America, engaging with spiritual classics in community by the year 2030. Will you join this growing community as we pursue God together by reading and discussing spiritual classics with gospel friends and kingdom coworkers.

A larger dream also informs Sacred Roots—a dream that imagines a million Christian workers equipped to serve among the global poor (Matt 9:36-38). The Center for the Study of Global Christianity reports that in the middle of 2020 there were approximately two and a half billion people living in urban poverty.[3] This number will increase to over four billion by the year 2050. Sacred Roots dreams of equipping one million Christian leaders among this great multitude—women and men like Prince Kaboo—with access to excellent editions of some of the greatest spiritual classics the Christian tradition has produced. Ultimately, the goal is increased faithfulness as leaders mature in representing Christ in local churches that are centered on Scripture, grounded in Nicene truth, and

---

3 For the most current statistics, see www.gordonconwell.edu/center-for-global-christianity/resources/status-of-global-christianity/.

engaged in contextually relevant witness to Christ's love in thousands of diverse contexts.[4]

Our Strategy: Scripture, Friendship and Spiritual Classics

Sacred Roots's strategy is simple. We believe fresh readings of Christian spiritual classics can lead Christian leaders into a deeper engagement with the God revealed in Scripture and into deeper friendships with one another.

Christian spiritual classics strengthen and deepen our roots in Scripture and help us produce the Spirit's fruit. One day Jesus asked a serious student of the Bible a simple question, *"How do you read it?"* (Luke 10:26). Of the more than three hundred questions asked by Jesus in the Gospels, few are more relevant today. Faithfulness in our generation demands that we learn to read Scripture in a way consistent with the foundational truths held by followers of Jesus in every culture since the first century. We read Christian spiritual classics to discover faithful and fruitful readings of Scripture. As Dr. Don Davis has noted, the church's "Great Tradition" perennially opens our eyes to new riches in Scripture's "Authoritative Tradition."[5]

A truth believed by all Christians, in all places, and at all times is that there is one God who exists as Father, Son, and Holy Spirit. From "before to beyond time," an eternal friendship between the Trinity's three persons has existed at the center of reality. Spiritual friendship provides the start and heart of truth. Just as spiritual classics can reveal new riches from Scripture, so they can help us grow in

---

4   Don Davis, *Sacred Roots: A Primer on Retrieving the Great Tradition* (Wichita, KS: The Urban Ministry Institute, 2010), 35–45.

5   Ibid.

love for God and neighbors. They can provide practical help in deepening our friendships with the Father, the Son, the Holy Spirit and with other believers—both with believers in this generation and with those surrounding us in the great cloud of witnesses (Heb 12:1; 13:7). Why do Christian leaders desperately need to pursue strong friendships? Start with these three reasons.

1. First, each of us has eyes far too small to see what God wants to show us! No one can begin to grasp the great things God is doing across 100 billion galaxies and throughout the many generations since the universe's creation. Friends, standing in different places provides additional eyes to see from different perspectives what God is doing in the world and across history.

2. Second, each of us battles a sinful nature that distorts our perception of the truth. We need friends who speak truth to us, sharpening us like iron sharpening iron (Prov 27:17).

3. Third, all of us view creation through a particular culture's time and place. Each culture exists with a unique version of virtue and vice. Friends who speak to us from other cultures and centuries often affirm virtues in our culture, but they can also reflect ways our culture's vice habitually offends against kingdom *shalom*.

In sum, Sacred Roots Spiritual Classics can help us grow in our friendship with God and neighbor (Matt 22:37–40). Neighbors include the living Christian leaders with whom we read and discuss this spiritual classic. However, "neighbor" also includes the author (or authors) of this spiritual classic. These women and men walked faithfully with God and neighbor. Their life and teachings produced good fruit in their generation and then continued to do so in the lives of other Christian leaders—often across many cultures and centuries. As an editorial team, we can personally testify to the fruitfulness of the time we have spent with our "friends," the "ancient witnesses" in the Sacred Roots Spiritual Classics. If you choose to invest in careful conversation with these saints of old (Heb 13:7), we are confident you will not only experience practical fruit in the present, but you will also gain new friends for eternity.

Tactical Notes: Christian Leaders Are Christian Readers

Throughout church history, fruitful Christian leaders have been intentional readers. Augustine (d. 430), a pastor and bishop in Africa, was challenged to a new level of ministry by reading a spiritual biography about an Egyptian Christian leader named Anthony (d. 356).[6] Protestant leaders like Martin Luther, John Calvin, John Wesley, Elizabeth Fry, Phoebe Palmer, and many others all published editions of spiritual classics for Christian leaders in their generation. Charles Harrison Mason (d. 1961), founder of the largest Pentecostal denomination in North America (Church of God in Christ), was called to ministry through a reading of the autobiography of missionary and evangelist Amanda Smith.[7] More recently, leaders like C. S. Lewis, A. W. Tozer, James Houston, and Rick Warren have

---

6   Athanasius of Alexandria, *On the Incarnation: The Good News of Jesus for the Renewal of the World*, ed. Jeremy Treat, Sacred Roots Spiritual Classics 6 (Upland, IN: Samuel Morris Publications, 2025).

7   Amanda Smith, *An Autobiography: The Story of the Lord's Dealings with Mrs. Amanda Smith, the Colored Evangelist; Containing an Account of Her Life Work of Faith, and Her Travels in America, England, Ireland, Scotland, India, and Africa, as an Independent Missionary* (Chicago: Meyer, 1893).

encouraged Christian leaders to read wisely, especially choosing Christian spiritual classics.[8]

How to Read the Text

Plan your reading. Reading a spiritual classic is a bit like reading your Bible. You can read it anywhere or anytime, but there are times and places that will position you to better receive insight and truth. SRSC readers tend to read each spiritual classic several times, and many will "read" it in both written and audiobook versions. We read to hear what the original author of the text is saying and to understand what the Holy Spirit might be directing our attention to hear or reflect upon. On your day of rest (Sabbath), reserve some time to read or at least set aside some time to plan when you will read from your spiritual classic that week. If you have a daily commute, perhaps use some of the time to listen and reflect on an audible version of the SRSC.

Work your reading plan. Once you have planned to read your spiritual classic, begin with the introduction. The introduction is written by a contemporary friend with significant ministry experience. This friend has spent much time reading and getting to know the spiritual classic and the author who wrote it. Often, the introduction is written by someone who has read the spiritual classic dozens of times. The introduction will help you get the most out of your first several readings of the text.

After reading the introduction, notice that all Sacred Roots Spiritual Classics are divided into eight chapters.

---

8 Explore the essays in Jamin Goggin and Kyle Strobel, eds., *Reading the Christian Spiritual Classics: A Guide for Evangelicals* (Downers Grove, IL: InterVarsity, 2013).

These chapters are not always of equal length, but they all are weighty enough to engage your head, heart, and hands as well as your habitat and habits. Following the eight chapters, every SRSC includes a short section called Continuing the Conversation. If you enjoyed reading the spiritual classic, then Continuing the Conversation will help you discover more resources to engage the author(s) of the spiritual classic.

The Sacred Roots Spiritual Classics are divided into ten parts to make it easier to talk about the text with friends and coworkers. The table below provides four examples of how to read a SRSC with a group of friends. When friends commit to read and discuss a SRSC together, the group is called a Sacred Roots Study Group.

SRSC Section to Read	"Sunday School" Class	"Church-Based Seminary" Module	Monthly Pastor's Meeting	Quarterly Retreat Discussion Group
	Ten Weeks	Eight Weeks	Monthly	Quarterly
Introduction	Week 1	Week 1	Month 1	Read text before retreat and then discuss
Ch. 1	Week 2			
Ch. 2	Week 3	Week 2		
Ch. 3	Week 4	Week 3		
Ch. 4	Week 5	Week 4	Month 2	
Ch. 5	Week 6	Week 5		
Ch. 6	Week 7	Week 6		
Ch. 7	Week 8	Week 7	Month 3	
Ch. 8	Week 9			
Afterword / Resources for Application	Week 10	Week 8		

Review your reading. The best readers, like the best leaders, do more than make a plan and work it. They also pause to take time to review their work—or in this case—their reading.[9] Robert Clinton has noted that only around 25

---

9 The PWR (Plan, Work, Review) process is explained further by Don Allsman, *The Heroic Venture: A Parable of Project Leadership* (Wichita, KS: The Urban Ministry

percent of leaders in the Bible finished well.[10] If we hope to finish well in our generation we must learn to *attend* to our habitat, our head, our heart, our hands, and our habits. To *attend* means to pay attention, to apply our self, to prioritize and to value something enough to give it our time and our energy. Each chapter concludes with five types of questions aimed at helping you review your progress toward finishing well and hearing Jesus say, "Well done, good and faithful servant" (Matt 25:23).

Habitat? Habitat questions ask us to pause and look around at our environment, our culture, our generation, our nationality, and the things that make up the *Zeitgeist* (spirit of the times). Questions may ask about the author's habitat or our own. Since the SRSC were written across many centuries and cultures, they often help us notice aspects of our culture needing attention.

Head? Auguste Rodin's sculpture known as *The Thinker* sits before an 18-feet-tall sculpture called *The Gates of Hell*. The massive sculptural group reflects Rodin's engagement with a spiritual classic by Dante, *The Divine Comedy*. Head questions require serious intellectual engagement as you talk with friends about the author's ideas, claims, and proposals.

Heart? In August of 1541, John Calvin wrote a letter to a friend with this promise: "When I remember that I am not my own, I offer up my heart presented as a sacrifice to God." Calvin's

---

Institute, 2006).

10 Robert Clinton, *The Making of a Leader: Recognizing the Lessons and Stages of Leadership Development*, rev. ed. (Colorado Springs, CO: NavPress, 2012), 185–87.

personal seal expressed this sincere desire. God not only owns our mind, but also our will and emotions. Heart questions will help you attend to the people and things to which you give your loves.

Hands? Albrecht Dürer sketched a drawing called *Study of the Hands of an Apostle* in the year 1508. The apostles were men of action, yet Dürer portrays the apostle's hands in prayer. The action to which SRSC call us are often surprising. Hands questions will challenge you to evaluate carefully what action you are to take after a particular reading.

Habits? Charlotte Mason (d. 1923) was a master teacher. She believed Christian formation must carefully attend to habit formation. Like laying railroad tracks, habit formation is hard work. But once laid, great work requires little effort just as railroad cars run smoothly on tracks. Habits questions challenge you to reflect on small daily or weekly actions that form your character and the character of those around you.

Reading with Friends

The Sacred Roots Spiritual Classics are not meant to be read alone; indeed, it is impossible to do so. Every time we open a SRSC we read a book that *has been read* by thousands of Christian leaders in previous generations, *is being read* by thousands of Christian leaders in our generation, and *will be read* (if the return of Christ tarries) by thousands of Christian leaders in generations after us. The readers before us have already finished their race. These thousands of Christian leaders read the text in hundreds of different cultures and across dozens of different generations. All these "friends" read this text with you now. As you read the SRSC, imagine yourself talking about *Benedict's Rule* (SRSC 2) with the reformer Martin Luther; or picture yourself discussing Madam Guyon's *A Short and Easy Method of Prayer* with the missionary Amy Carmichael. Remember you never read a Sacred Roots Spiritual Classic alone.

However, it is not just leaders who have gone before, it is also leaders in the present with whom you must imagine reading this SRSC. Whatever benefit you find in reading will be doubled when you share it with a friend. Whatever trouble or difficulty you find in reading the text will be halved when you share it with a friend. Resolve to never read a Sacred Roots Spiritual Classic alone.

Perhaps you have noticed that the word "generation" has already appeared in this preface more than fifteen times? The SRSC represent the work of many generations working together. Five generations of evangelicals have worked and prayed together on this project since its public commencement in 2018. But these five generations of living evangelicals represent only a small sample of the many generations who have tested the faithfulness and fruitfulness of the SRSC. Why does this matter? In part, it matters because these texts are treasures to use and then pass on to the next generation of leaders. Recognize the emerging leaders God has called you to serve and steward—share the Sacred Roots Spiritual Classics with them.

Careful readers of Scripture know that the most influential leaders among God's people have always worked in teams. King David's teams became legends—"the three," "the thirty." The list of Paul's missionary and ministry team members whose names we know from the New Testament runs to nearly one hundred. Our Sacred Roots team of teams prays that this text will be a blessing and a reliable resource for you and your gospel friends as you pursue kingdom business together.

Grace and Peace,

Don, Uche, Greg, May, Ryan, Isaiah, and Hank

The Nicene Creed with Scriptural Support

The Urban Ministry Institute

We believe in one God,
Deut 6:4–5; Mark 12:29; 1 Cor 8:6

the Father Almighty,
Gen 17:1; Dan 4:35; Matt 6:9; Eph 4:6; Rev 1:8

Maker of heaven and earth
Gen 1:1; Isa 40:28; Rev 10:6

and of all things visible and invisible.
Ps 148; Rom 11:36; Rev 4:11

We believe in one Lord Jesus Christ, the only Begotten Son of God, begotten of the Father before all ages, God from God, Light from Light, True God from True God, begotten not created, of the same essence as the Father,
John 1:1–2; 3:18; 8:58; 14:9–10; 20:28; Col 1:15, 17; Heb 1:3–6

through whom all things were made.
John 1:3; Col 1:16

Who for us men and for our salvation came down from heaven and was incarnate by the Holy Spirit and the Virgin Mary and became human.
Matt 1:20–23; Luke 19:10; John 1:14; 6:38

Who for us too, was crucified under Pontius Pilate, suffered and was buried.
Matt 27:1–2; Mark 15:24–39, 43–47; Acts 13:29; Rom 5:8; Heb 2:10; 13:12

The third day he rose again according to the Scriptures,
Mark 16:5–7; Luke 24:6–8; Acts 1:3; Rom 6:9; 10:9; 2 Tim 2:8

ascended into heaven, and is seated at the right hand of the Father.
Mark 16:19; Eph 1:19–20

He will come again in glory to judge the living and the dead, and his Kingdom will have no end.
Isa 9:7; Matt 24:30; John 5:22; Acts 1:11; 17:31; Rom 14:9; 2 Cor 5:10; 2 Tim 4:1

We believe in the Holy Spirit, the Lord and life-giver,
Gen 1:1–2; Job 33:4; Pss 104:30; 139:7–8; Luke 4:18–19; John 3:5–6; Acts 1:1–2; 1 Cor 2:11; Rev 3:22

who proceeds from the Father and the Son,
John 14:16–18, 26; 15:26; 20:22

who together with the Father and Son is worshiped and glorified,
Isa 6:3; Matt 28:19; 2 Cor 13:14; Rev 4:8

who spoke by the prophets.
Num 11:29; Mic 3:8; Acts 2:17–18; 2 Pet 1:21

We believe in one holy, catholic, and apostolic Church.
Matt 16:18; 1 Cor 1:2; 10:17; Eph 5:25–28; 1 Tim 3:15; Rev 7:9

We acknowledge one baptism for the forgiveness of sin,
Acts 22:16; Eph 4:4–5; 1 Pet 3:21

And we look for the resurrection of the dead and the life of the age to come.
Isa 11:6–10; Mic 4:1–7; Luke 18:29–30; Rev 21:1–5; 21:22–22:5

Amen.

Memory Verses

Below are suggested memory verses, one for each section of the Creed.

The Father

Rev 4:11 (ESV) — Worthy are you, our Lord and God, to receive glory and honor and power, for you created all things, and by your will they existed and were created.

The Son

John 1:1 (ESV) — In the beginning was the Word, and the Word was with God, and the Word was God.

The Son's Mission

1 Cor 15:3–5 (ESV) — For what I received I passed on to you as of first importance: that Christ died for our sins according to the Scriptures, that he was buried, that he was raised on the third day according to the Scriptures, and that he appeared to Peter, and then to the Twelve.

The Holy Spirit

Rom 8:11 (ESV) — If the Spirit of him who raised Jesus from the dead dwells in you, he who raised Christ Jesus from the dead will also give life to your mortal bodies through his Spirit who dwells in you.

The Church

1 Pet 2:9 (ESV) — But you are a chosen race, a royal priesthood, a holy nation, a people for his own possession, that you may proclaim the excellencies of him who called you out of darkness into his marvelous light.

Our Hope

1 Thess 4:16–17 (ESV) — For the Lord himself will descend from heaven with a cry of command, with the voice of an archangel, and with the sound of the trumpet of God. And the dead in Christ will rise first. Then we who are alive, who are left, will be caught up together with them in the clouds to meet the Lord in the air, and so we will always be with the Lord.

From Before to Beyond Time:
The Plan of God and Human History

Adapted from Suzanne de Dietrich. *God's Unfolding Purpose*. Philadelphia: Westminster Press, 1976.

I. Before Time (Eternity Past)

1 Cor. 2:7 (ESV) – But we impart a secret and hidden wisdom of God, which God decreed before the ages for our glory (cf. Titus 1:2).

A. The Eternal Triune God
B. God's Eternal Purpose
C. The Mystery of Iniquity
D. The Principalities and Powers

II. Beginning of Time (Creation and Fall)

Gen. 1:1 (ESV) – In the beginning, God created the heavens and the earth.

A. Creative Word
B. Humanity
C. Fall
D. Reign of Death and First Signs of Grace

III. Unfolding of Time (God's Plan Revealed through Israel)

Gal. 3:8 (ESV) – And the Scripture, foreseeing that God would justify the Gentiles by faith, preached the Gospel beforehand to Abraham, saying, "In you shall all the nations be blessed" (cf. Rom. 9:4-5).

A. Promise (Patriarchs)
B. Exodus and Covenant at Sinai
C. Promised Land
D. The City, the Temple, and the Throne (Prophet, Priest, and King)
E. Exile
F. Remnant

Resources for Application 213

IV. Fullness of Time (Incarnation of the Messiah)

Gal. 4:4-5 (ESV) – But when the fullness of time had come, God sent forth his Son, born of woman, born under the law, to redeem those who were under the law, so that we might receive adoption as sons.

A. The King Comes to His Kingdom
B. The Present Reality of His Reign
C. The Secret of the Kingdom: the Already and the Not Yet
D. The Crucified King
E. The Risen Lord

V. The Last Times (The Descent of the Holy Spirit)

Acts 2:16-18 (ESV) – But this is what was uttered through the prophet Joel: "'And in the last days it shall be,' God declares, 'that I will pour out my Spirit on all flesh, and your sons and your daughters shall prophesy, and your young men shall see visions, and your old men shall dream dreams; even on my male servants and female servants in those days I will pour out my Spirit, and they shall prophesy.'"

A. Between the Times: the Church as Foretaste of the Kingdom
B. The Church as Agent of the Kingdom
C. The Conflict Between the Kingdoms of Darkness and Light

VI. The Fulfillment of Time (The Second Coming)

Matt. 13:40-43 (ESV) – Just as the weeds are gathered and burned with fire, so will it be at the close of the age. The Son of Man will send his angels, and they will gather out of his Kingdom all causes of sin and all lawbreakers, and throw them into the fiery furnace. In that place there will be weeping and gnashing of teeth. Then the righteous will shine like the sun in the Kingdom of their Father. He who has ears, let him hear.

A. The Return of Christ
B. Judgment
C. The Consummation of His Kingdom

VII. Beyond Time (Eternity Future)

1 Cor. 15:24-28 (ESV) – Then comes the end, when he delivers the Kingdom to God the Father after destroying every rule and every authority and power. For he must reign until he has put all his enemies under his feet. The last enemy to be destroyed is death. For "God has put all things in subjection under his feet." But when it says, "all things are put in subjection," it is plain that he is excepted who put all things in subjection under him. When all things are subjected to him, then the Son himself will also be subjected to him who put all things in subjection under him, that God may be all in all.

A. Kingdom Handed Over to God the Father
B. God as All in All

About the Sacred Roots Project

Sacred Roots seeks to equip and empower under-resourced congregational leaders in urban, rural, and incarcerated communities. One avenue for accomplishing this goal is the Sacred Roots Spiritual Classics, a series of Christian spiritual classics that equip congregational leaders to engage the wealth of the Great Tradition.

The Sacred Roots Spiritual Classics include:

Praying the Psalms with Augustine and Friends
   Edited by Carmen Joy Imes

Becoming a Community of Disciples:
Guidelines from Abbot Benedict and Bishop Basil
   Benedict of Nursia and Basil of Caesarea, edited by Greg Peters

Spiritual Friendship:
Learning How to Be Friends with God and One Another
   Aelred of Rievaulx, edited by Hank Voss

Christian Mission and Poverty:
Wisdom from 2,000 Years of Church Leaders
   Edited by Andrew T. Draper

Books Jesus Read: Learning from the Apocrypha
   Edited by Robert F. Lay

On the Incarnation:
The Good News of Jesus for the Renewal of the World
   Athanasius of Alexandria, edited by Jeremy Treat

First Christian Voices: Practices of the Apostolic Fathers
   Edited by Michael Cooper

Las Casas on Faithful Witness
   Bartolomé de las Casas, edited by Robert Chao Romero and Marcos Canales

Reading the Bible Spiritually:
Guidance from Guigo II, Reformers, and Puritans
   Edited by Greg Peters

The Pursuit of God
   A. W. Tozer, edited by Glen G. Scorgie

Pulpit Spirituality:
Jonathan Edwards on Soul Work and Soul Care
   Jonathan Edwards, edited by Kyle Strobel and Kenneth P. Minkema

Mission with Prophetic Power:
The Journal of John Woolman
   John Woolman, edited by Evan B. Howard

Reading the Bible to Meet Jesus:
Demonstration of the Apostolic Preaching
   Irenaeus of Lyons, edited by Gregory S. MaGee

Killing Sin:
Lessons on Holiness from John Owen and Phoebe Palmer
   John Owen and Phoebe Palmer, edited by Daniel Hill

The Interior Castle:
Learning to Pray with Teresa of Ávila
   Teresa of Ávila, edited by Nancy Reyes Frazier

God Is Faithful Still:
The Autobiography of George Müller
  George Müller, edited by Uche Anizor

The Editorial Team of the Sacred Roots Spiritual Classics includes:

Rev. Dr. Don Davis
Publisher
The Urban Ministry Institute

Rev. Dr. Hank Voss
Executive Editor
Taylor University

Dr. Uche Anizor
Senior Editor
Biola University, Talbot School of Theology

Rev. Dr. Greg Peters
Senior Editor
Biola University, Torrey Honors College

Dr. May Young
Senior Editor
Taylor University

Rev. Ryan Carter
Managing Editor
The Urban Ministry Institute

Isaiah Swain
Managing Editor
Taylor University

The Editorial Team acknowledges and appreciates Dr. Gwenfair Adams (Gordon-Conwell Theological Seminary), Dr. Betsy Barber (Biola University), Rev. Dr. Nigel Black (Winslow Baptist Church), Dr. Jonathan Calvillo (Boston University School of Divinity), Dr. Laura Edwards (Taylor University), Rev. Nathan Esla (Lutheran Bible Translators), Dr. Nancy Frazier (Dallas Theological Seminary), Dr. Jeff Greenman (Regent College), Dr. Kevin Hector (University of Chicago Divinity School), Rev. Dr. Wil Hernandez (Centerquest), Dr. James Houston (Regent College), Dr. Evan B. Howard (Spirituality Shoppe), Rev. Susie Krehbiel (Missionary, Retired), Rev. Dr. Tim Larsen (Wheaton College), Dr. Stephanie Lowery (Africa International University), Dr. Daniel Owens (Hanoi Bible College), Rev. Dr. Oscar Owens (West Angeles Church of God), Dr. Bob Priest (Taylor University), Rev. Dr. Robert Chao Romero (University of California, Los Angeles), Rev. Dr. Jerry Root (Wheaton College), Dr. Fred Sanders (Biola University), Dr. Glen G. Scorgie (Bethel University), Dr. Kyle Strobel (Biola University), Dr. Daniel Treier (Wheaton College), and Dr. Kevin Vanhoozer (Trinity Evangelical Divinity School) for their support and encouragement. Artwork throughout the Sacred Roots Spiritual Classics is illustrated by Naomi Noyes.

The Sacred Roots Spiritual Classics are dedicated to all Christian leaders who have loved the poor and recognized the importance of Christian spiritual classics for nurturing the next generation. We especially recognize these fourteen:

John Wesley (1703–1791)

Rebecca Protten (1718–1780)

Elizabeth Fry (1780–1845)

Phoebe Palmer (1807–1874)

Dora Yu (1873–1931)

A. W. Tozer (1897–1963)

Howard Thurman (1899–1981)

Watchman Nee (1903–1972)

James Houston (1922–)

J. I. Packer (1926–2020)

Tom Oden (1931–2016)

René Padilla (1932–2021)

Dallas Willard (1935–2013)

Bruce Demarest (1935–2021)

Remember your leaders,
those who spoke to you the word of God.
Consider the outcome of their way of life,
and imitate their faith.
~ Hebrews 13:7

THEOLOGY & ETHICS

Scripture Index

Genesis
1:1, 27, 208, 212
1:1–2, 209
1:3, 156
2:16–17, 28
17:1, 208
25:27, 129
49:10, 95

Exodus
32:32, 163
33:13, 163

Numbers
11:29, 209
24:5–7, 84
24:17, 84

Deuteronomy
6:4–5, 208
28:66, 86, 90

Joshua
23:14, 146

1 Samuel
17, 194

2 Samuel
15:31, 169

Nehemiah
9:6–38, 193

Job
33:4, 209
40:16, 133

Psalms

1, 168, 169, 170, 174
2, 157, 168, 169, 170, 173, 174
3, 164, 167, 169, 170
4, 168, 169, 170
5, 167, 169, 170, 173
6, 167, 169, 170
7, 167, 169, 170
8, 168, 170
9, 158, 167, 168, 170, 172
10, 167, 168, 170, 172
11, 170
12, 164, 167, 170
13, 167, 170
14, 168, 170
15, 170
16, 167, 173
17, 164, 167, 170
18, 168, 170
19, 153, 166, 170
20, 155, 168, 170
21, 167, 173
22, 157, 167, 173
22:16–18, 86
23, 168, 170
24, 153, 158, 170, 172, 173
24:7, 68
25, 167, 170
26, 167, 170
27, 168, 170
27:3, 137
28, 154, 167, 170
29, 154, 167, 171
30, 171
31, 167, 171
32, 168, 169, 170, 171
33, 167, 171
33:6, 156
34, 168, 171
34:14, 160
35, 167, 170
36, 168, 171
37, 167, 171
37:8, 160
38, 167, 169, 170
39, 168, 171
40, 168, 171
41, 168, 169, 170, 171
42, 168, 171
43, 167, 170
44, 166, 171
45, 155, 156, 167, 173
46, 168, 171
46:10, 150
47, 158, 167, 173
48, 168, 172
49, 166
50, 155, 158, 166, 173
51, 164, 171, 194
52, 168, 171
53, 168, 170

54, 164, 167, 171
55, 167, 171
56, 164, 167, 171
57, 164, 167, 171
57:2, 192
58, 168, 171
59, 167, 171
60, 167
61, 167
62, 168, 171
63, 168, 171
64, 167, 168, 171
65, 168, 171
66, 168, 171
67, 172
68, 167
68:1–2, 142
69, 157, 167, 173
70, 167, 171
71, 167, 171
72, 157, 158, 173
73, 166, 172
74, 167, 172
75, 167, 169, 170, 172
76, 167, 168, 172
77, 166, 168, 172
78, 154, 166, 171, 193
79, 167, 172
80, 167
81, 167, 168, 172
82, 158, 168
82:6–7, 33

83, 167, 172
84, 168, 170, 172
85, 168, 172
86, 167, 170, 172
87, 156
88, 157, 167, 170
89, 166, 171
90, 166, 167, 170
90:1, 192
91, 168, 172
92, 167, 172
93, 172, 173
94, 172
95, 167, 172
96, 167, 172, 173
97, 167, 168, 172
98, 167, 173
99, 168, 173
100, 169, 172
101, 172
102, 167, 172
103, 167, 173
104, 167, 173
104:30, 209
105, 154, 167, 168, 171, 172, 173, 193
106, 154, 167, 171, 172, 173, 193
107, 154, 155, 166, 167, 171, 172, 173
107:20, 95
108, 167, 168, 172

Psalms, cont.
109, 167, 173
110, 155, 158, 167, 173
111, 167, 172, 173
112, 168, 173
113, 168, 173
114, 154, 166, 167, 168, 171, 173
115, 154, 166, 168, 171, 173
116, 168, 169, 170, 173
117, 168, 173
118, 155, 167, 172, 173
118:7, 135
118:10, 142
118:27, 95
119, 168, 169, 170, 173
119:105, 184
120–134, 155, 173, 190
121, 168
122, 155, 168
123, 167
124, 168
125, 168
126, 155, 168, 172
127, 166, 171
128, 168, 169, 170
129, 168
130, 167
131, 167
132, 167
133, 168
135, 168, 173
136, 167, 172, 173, 193
137, 166, 173
138, 157, 167, 172
139, 167, 173
139:7–8, 209
140, 167, 173
141, 170
142, 164, 167, 171
143, 167, 173
144, 168, 173
145, 168, 173
146, 168, 173
147, 168, 173
148, 168, 173, 208
149, 173
150, 167, 168, 173
151, 168

Proverbs
27:17, 199

Isaiah
1:16, 159
2:4, 116
6:3, 209
7:14, 84
8:4, 74
9:7, 209
11:6–10, 209
11:9, 107
11:10, 86
19:1, 84

35:3–6, 92
36–37, 159
40:28, 208
53:3–5, 85
53:4, 157
53:6–8, 85
53:8, 90
53:8–10, 86
63:9, 95
65:1–2, 91

Jeremiah
4:14, 159
11:19, 86

Ezekiel
11:19, 178
36:26, 178

Daniel
3, 193
4:35, 208
9:24–25, 93
12, 159

Hosea
4:12, 134
11:1, 84

Micah
3:8, 209
4:1–7, 209

Matthew
1:5, 194
1:20–23, 208
1:23, 84
4:4, 183
4:20, 130
6:7, 131
6:9, 185, 208
6:10, 192
6:16, 185
6:34, 130
9:36–38, 197
9:38, 195
11:13, 95
11:29, 165
12:36, 169
13:40–43, 213
16:18, 209
19:4, 26
19:6, 27
19:21, 130
19:28, 178
22:37–40, 199
24:30, 209
24:42, 124
25:23, 204
26:64, 124
27:1–2, 208
28:19, 209

Mark

3:31–35, 178
5:7, 81
12:29, 208
15:24–39, 208
15:43–47, 208
16:5–7, 209
16:19, 209

Luke

1:28, 156
4:18–19, 209
4:34, 79
6:12–13, 132, 190
9:23, 145, 146
10:18, 68
10:26, 198
18:29–30, 209
19:10, 50, 52, 208
24:6–8, 209

John

1, 24
1:1, 210
1:1–2, 156, 208
1:1–3, 29
1:3, 27, 208
1:14, 24, 156, 208
1:18, 9
2:1–11, 56
3:3, 50
3:5–6, 209
3:16, 60
3:18, 208
3:31, 120
5:22, 209
6:38, 208
8:58, 208
9:32–33, 93
10:37–38, 55
12:6, 192
12:32, 59, 68
14–17, 194
14:9–10, 208
14:16–18, 209
14:26, 209
15, 192
15:26, 209
16:33, 9
20:22, 209
20:28, 208

Acts

1:1–2, 209
1:3, 209
1:8, 195
1:11, 209
2:16–18, 213
2:17–18, 209
4:23–32, 174
4:35, 130
13:29, 208
13:36, 192, 194
17:28, 101
17:31, 209
22:16, 209

Romans

1:25, 46
1:26–27, 34
5:3–5, 161
5:8, 208
6:9, 209
6:13, 193
8, 193
8:3–4, 135
8:11, 210
8:32, 143
8:35, 137
9:4–5, 211
10:9, 209
11:36, 208
12:2, 178
14:9, 209

1 Corinthians

1:2, 209
1:21, 51
2:7, 212
2:8, 118
2:9, 125
2:11, 209
4:1, 194
8:6, 208
9:27, 135
10:17, 209
11:1, 165
15:1–4, 182
15:2, 182
15:3–5, 210
15:10, 134
15:21–22, 44
15:24–28, 214
15:53–55, 61
15:55, 73

2 Corinthians

1:20, 97
4:16, 178
5:10, 124, 209
5:14–15, 44
5:17, 13, 126
12:10, 136
13:14, 209

Galatians

1:9, 162
2:20, 82
3:8, 212
3:13, 66
4:4–5, 213
5–6, 193

Ephesians

1:19–20, 209
2:2, 59, 68
2:14, 66
3:17–19, 52
4:4–5, 209
4:6, 208
5:25–28, 209
6:11, 135

Philippians
3:13, 136
4:4, 162

Colossians
1:15, 208
1:16, 208
1:17, 208
2:15, 108
3:10, 11, 178

1 Thessalonians
4:16–17, 211
5:17, 131
5:18, 161, 185

2 Thessalonians
3:10, 131
1 Timothy
3:15, 209
4:16, 13
6:15, 45

2 Timothy
1:10, 11
2:8, 209
3:12, 161
3:16, 151, 153, 183
4:1, 209

Titus
1:2, 212

Hebrews
1:3–6, 208
2:9, 44
2:10, 44, 208
2:14, 44
2:14–15, 61
4:12, 78
10:20, 68
11, 193
11:3, 27
11:35, 194
12:1, 199
12:1–3, 147
12:2, 182
13:7, 199, 200
13:12, 208

James
2:25, 194

1 Peter
2:9, 210
2:22, 54
3:21, 209

2 Peter
1:4, 11, 119
1:21, 209
1 John
1:9, 37

Revelation
 1:8, 208
 3:22, 209
 4:8, 209
 4:11, 208, 210
 7:9, 209
 10:6, 208
 21:1–5, 209
 21:22–22:5, 209
 22:1–4, 126
 22:20, 126

www.ingramcontent.com/pod-product-compliance
Lightning Source LLC
Chambersburg PA
CBHW071113160426
43196CB00013B/2557